Rendezvous in Cyprus

BY THE SAME AUTHOR

A Fool on Wheels
A Fool in the Desert
A Fool Strikes Oil
Columbus was Right!
In Search of Sheba
The Way of the Chariots
The Highway of the Three Kings

BARBARA TOY

Rendezvous in Cyprus

JOHN MURRAY

Printed in Great Britain
by Cox & Wyman Ltd, London
Fakenham and Reading
0 7195 2074 6

TO MARIE LOUISE

'I am not sure that what I feel is remorse. I have seen the ocean when lashed by something in itself or out of itself, it wrecked and ruined; and I have seen the ocean when it carried my barque to safety. It was the same ocean, and what is the use of words?'

Contents

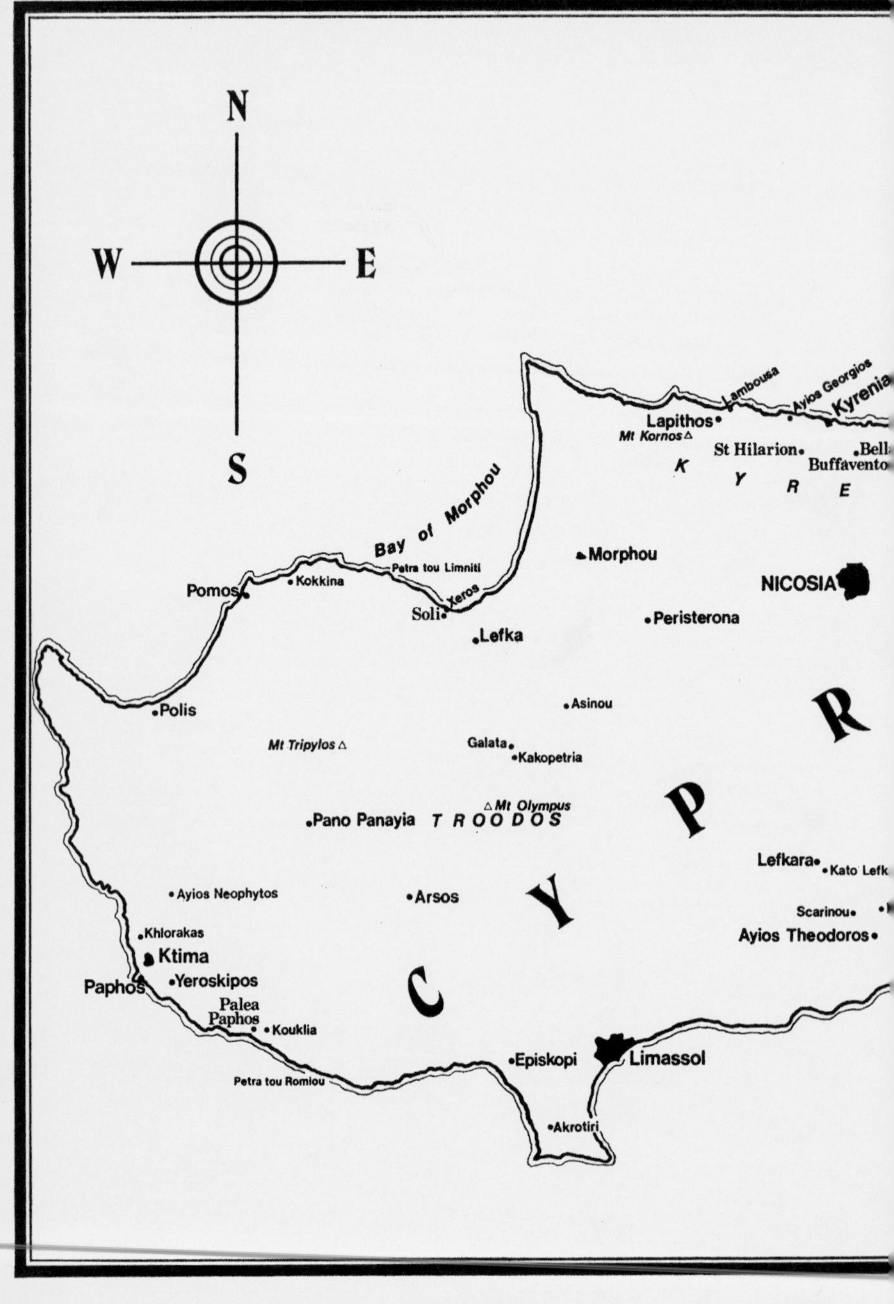

N
W
E
S
Lambousa
Ayios Georgios
Kyrenia
Lapithos
Mt Kornos
St Hilarion
Buffavento
K Y R E
Bay of Morphou
Morphou
NICOSIA
Petra tou Limniti
Pomos
Kokkina
Xeros
Soli
Lefka
Peristerona
Polis
Asinou
R
Mt Tripylos
Galata
Kakopetria
Mt Olympus
Pano Panayia
T R O O D O S
P
Lefkara
Ayios Neophytos
Arsos
Y
Scarinou
Ayios Theodoros
Khlorakas
Ktima
Paphos
Yeroskipos
C
Palea Paphos
Kouklia
Episkopi
Limassol
Petra tou Romiou
Akrotiri

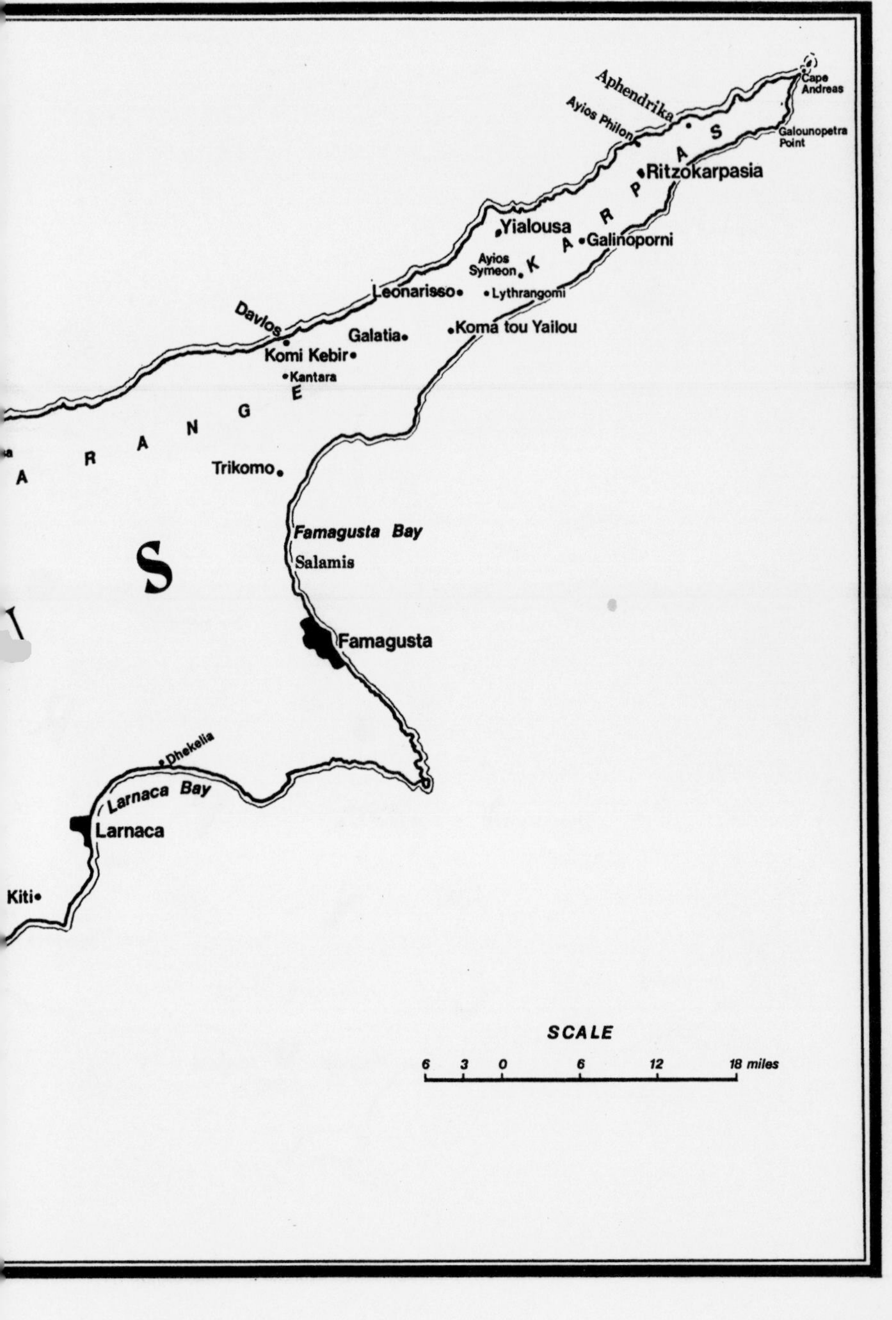

Cape Andreas
Aphendrika
Ayios Philon
Galounopetra Point
KARPAS
Ritzokarpasia
Yialousa
Galinoporni
Ayios Symeon
Leonarisso
Lythrangomi
Davlos
Galatia
Koma tou Yailou
Komi Kebir
Kantara
A RANGE
Trikomo
S
Famagusta Bay
Salamis
Famagusta
Dhekelia
Larnaca Bay
Larnaca
Kiti
SCALE
6 3 0 6 12 18 miles

Illustrations

Photographs by the author

Prelude

Friendship comes at unexpected times and from the most diverse quarters. Sometimes it matures after many years and at other times – and this is just as strong – it is born immediately at a chance meeting. The latter kind often has to endure long separations over the subsequent years. Such was my friendship with Belkiss whom I met on the first journey, with my Land-Rover in Cyprus in the spring of 1951. During the intervening years I continued to travel and she married, had children and settled into her own life. Now I was returning to Cyprus where we hoped to meet.

To Cyprus also many things had happened during that time, the island had gained independence and was experiencing some of the trials that such a state can bring, not least was the estrangement between the two communities of Greek and Turkish Cypriots. I was looking forward to seeing its new-found prosperity despite these troubles, and to revisit many places we had seen previously. The beauty of the island drew me, my friendship with Kiss was the spur.

This time I was coming the easy way, arriving with the Land-Rover by ship from England, but during the voyage the whole scene changed when Cyprus hit the world headlines with the Ayios Theodoros–Kophinou incident and massacre of November 1967. Tension ran high, a special meeting of the U.N. Security Council was called and the island came nearer to full-scale war than she ever had before. Now it would surely be a very different place from the pleasure-loving island I had known previously. I hoped to be able to stay long enough to see a return to a more normal state of affairs. And yet – it has been said that Cyprus is its own destruction, and for how long in its chequered history has the Cypriot been allowed peace. . . .?

I

Returning

Even though you tie a hundred knots – the string remains one. RUMI

'Of course it was disappointing that you weren't at Famagusta to meet me. It would have been grand if, having seen me off all those years ago, you were standing there near Othello's Tower with a welcome. As it was the whole place was heavy with this awful emergency and it was necessary for me to play it cool, excite no interest and just drive off . . . some of the things I have learnt about travelling during the intervening years since we met. As it was it all went smoothly and then quite unaccountably I drove across the Kyrenia Range and arrived here, not far from the spot of the ancient Aphrodisium which was a coincidence as I have come to look for her. Come when you can, if you can . . .'

The rift between Turkish and Greek Cypriots blows up into near civil war from time to time and the United Nations Peace Keeping Force could almost be a permanent fixture. The recent flare-up with its resulting massacres which happened just eight days previously, the presence of not only the UNFICYP troops but thousands of Greek and Turkish soldiers from the mainland, as well as the imposed curfew, made me wonder if I would be allowed to drive round the island in my Land-Rover or even to land. However, with a lack of fuss and a lot of common sense, the customs officials cleared the vehicle and I was free to leave the port in less than an hour. There may be trouble farther along the coast with the resulting scars, but here life seemed very normal. A dark young man in European suit and speaking excellent English, 'saw me through'.

'Come,' he said finally, 'I shall show you where the shipping company's agent is, not far from the dock gates.' He followed me out to the Land-Rover. 'They will give you all the information about the island.'

We drove along the quay but when we reached the gates, my companion stopped me.

'This is as far as I go,' he said with a slightly embarrassed air and pointed to a white building diagonally opposite. 'The agent is over there.' As he climbed out of the Land-Rover he paused, and then continued by way of explanation, 'You see, I am a Turkish Cypriot and I don't go into the Greek quarter.'

'Although you work amongst them?'

He nodded. 'We get on well. I went to school with some of them. But I go to our own quarter in the old city through the sea gate each evening, and they leave by this one.' He grinned, 'I know, it's crazy!' He shrugged and added. 'Do come and see me when you are back in Famagusta and I'll show you the old part inside the walls, it is quite the most interesting.'

'I shall take you up on that,' I said and watched the trim figure as he disappeared amongst the mixed crowd on the quayside. Crazy is right!

Old Famagusta has massive walls and a dry moat. It is occupied entirely by Turkish Cypriots and most of them live within the walls. West of the city and along the coast is Varosha which used to be a small village; now it has become the main part of modern Famagusta and the administration centre for the Greek Cypriots. The long sandy beach is backed by large hotels and apartment houses and the town is growing fast. In the centre there are already traffic problems, for there has been little town planning.

The contrast in crossing the fosse into the Turkish quarter from this busy part of the town, is very great. The solid Venetian walls and bastions enclose a cluttered city of narrow alleyways and ancient buildings, many of them in ruins. The fine façade of the Cathedral of St Nicholas which is now a mosque, overlooks the empty square, although much of the rest of the building has been damaged by earthquakes and during the notorious siege of 1571. The old city is curiously quiet for until recently there were restrictions imposed on the Turkish Cypriots for the purchase of vehicles, petrol and materials for building. Nearer the sea, fewer buildings have been left standing and the citadel and tower of Othello overlook the modern harbour.

It was already afternoon. Where should I go? It was better not to make too many inquiries for I might be 'handed over to the authorities'. My British-registered Land-Rover was easily recognizable and I hoped this labelled me neutral. It was Saturday and a bad day to arrive in the capital, Nicosia, so I returned through the high-arched gate, crossed the fosse, and turned to the east along the coast road. At the first junction there was a UNFICYP observation post, a small pale blue box flying the U.N. flag of the same colour. These little specks of blue became a very familiar sight during the months that followed. A bronzed Swedish soldier waved and beyond, in a compound, some more soldiers, stripped to the waist, were playing a ball game. The sunlight, the bronzed men and the pale blue gave a slightly musical comedy air.

Flat broken ground ran to the sea to my right, and ahead – mauve and blue in the distance – was the outline of the Kyrenia Range.

* * * *

Disraeli said that Cyprus was the key to western Asia, for it lies little more than forty miles from Turkey and seventy-six miles from Syria; but modern transport and international organizations make such a generalization unnecessary today. However, it certainly came in for a lot of attention from both East and West during their continuous struggles for supremacy in this part of the world. Twice the island was given away as a gift – by Julius Caesar to Ptolemy and Arsinoe, and later Anthony bestowed it upon Cleopatra. Before this time it had been divided into nine kingdoms, then the Egyptians, followed by the Romans, took over. Next came the Greek Emperors of Constantinople, who after a lull of nearly two hundred years suffered many onslaughts by the Arabs but later Isaac, Duke of Comneni, proclaimed himself Emperor and reigned in absolute possession until 1191 when Richard Coeur de Lion, on his way to the Third Crusade attacked and finally captured both the island and Isaac. This digression occurred because of an insult by Isaac to Richard's fiancée Berengaria of Navarre when her ship sought shelter in the port of Limassol. Later Richard sold the island to the Knights Templars on a time-payment basis, but they found it too expensive and tried to sell it back to him. Finally it was made over to Guy de Lusignan; and so began the three-hundred-year rule by the House of Lusignan that has left so many beautiful, if entirely Latin traces in the castles and churches which they built and decorated.

And what of the local inhabitants during these centuries of land grabbing? If the Lusignan rule and way of life was brilliant, they remained mere vassals and no doubt regretted the easier home rule of Byzantium. The island continued to attract attention, for the Crusaders, many having lost their original goal of the Holy Places, were looking for other lands to conquer and to settle. Cyprus, with its riches and its position was also more stable than the mainland and they flocked here, so that the port of Famagusta became the centre of Eastern trade. The town acquired a great reputation as a growing number of men of letters settled here from all over Europe. Already the cathedrals of Nicosia, Famagusta, the castles of St Hilarion, Buffavento and Kantara, and the Abbey of Bellapais, were well known. Famous writers dedicated works to the kings of the island and by the fourteenth century the merchants and citizens were living in such wealth and luxury that western travellers all commented on it. The jewels worn by the women and the dowries given far exceeded those of the courts of Europe.

Beneath this spectacular façade the peasants remained poor and the Orthodox Bishops were reduced to dependence on the Latin Bishops; a state which continued until the arrival of the Turks who revived the Orthodox Church as a piece of political strategy.

The rule of the Lusignans was coming to a close in 1460 when Charlotte, the rightful heir, was expelled by her bastard half-brother James, who was the son of the king's mistress Marietta. James married Catherine Cornaro, the daughter of a Venetian nobleman and the Republic made her a 'daughter of Venice', with an eye to the territorial gains likely to result from such a union. When both James and his one-year-old son had died, Catherine ruled under the wing of Venice. In 1489 she was forcibly persuaded to abdicate in favour of Venice; and so the island came under the Republic's direct rule.

Although they had gone to great lengths to gain control of the island, the Venetians looked on it chiefly as a military post which would help them stem the attacks and growing menace of the Turks. They took little interest in the island except to build and strengthen fortifications and to enjoy the luxurious living for which it was famous. They also drew what revenue they could from the already impoverished islanders and for this reason there was a general apathy amongst the natives. Trade decreased and the corruption which was already beginning to appear in Venice was felt here also. Such was the state of the island when in 1571 the Ottomans invaded and laid siege to Nicosia and Famagusta. It is no wonder the Ottomans were welcomed by the Cypriot peasants when the Latin priests were expelled and the Greek Orthodox Church restored. (It is ironical to note that two hundred years later the church had become so influential that the alarmed Turks arrested and executed the Archbishop and leading personages of the church on charges of helping Greece in her struggle for independence).

The Turkish Government was inept and except for the reforms instituted by Sultan Mahmud II in 1838, which brought a small measure of prosperity, the island failed to regain its former wealth. By the Anglo-Turkish Convention of 4th June 1878, the island was handed over to be administered by Britain; and this state of affairs remained until the entry of Turkey into World War I when Cyprus was annexed by the British Crown.

In 1960 when the island became independent, the population, which consisted roughly of four-fifths Greek and one-fifth Turkish Cypriots, ruled their own country for the first time. The island has progressed since then, despite the unrest and near civil war between the two communities. It now has the highest standard of living, apart from Israel, in the Eastern Mediterranean and receives revenue from the British Sovereign Base, the United Nations Peace Keeping Force's personnel and the steadily increasing tourist trade, to say nothing of the large asbestos, copper, wine and fruit exports. The recollections of my first visit are very vivid for the island is beautiful and as exotic as the names it acquired during its chequered history – Acamantis, Aspelia, Amanthusia, Aerosa, Paphos, Salamina and Cythera to name but a few. The sun – now the most costly commodity in northern Europe – shines most of the time; income tax is not as crippling as our own and there is talk of its being reduced!

*　　*　　*　　*

I turned off the main road and ran towards an area that had a shanty town appearance, and the inhabitants the unmistakable look of gypsies. When I stopped to inquire the whereabouts of the house of Miss Mogabgab, they regarded me suspiciously. Finally a very old woman, gregarious and bored no doubt by the lack of new faces, pushed forward and directed me towards the rocky headland beyond. But firstly wouldn't I stay for some coffee, perhaps? She pleaded. But I left the row of sullen faces and drove towards a slight rise where a contingent of U.N. boys had a small camp. Nearer the seashore and standing alone was an enclosure surrounded by a high wall with iron gates that were closed and padlocked. Beyond the gates a long avenue of huge aloes led to a low house. It was the residence of Theophilus Mogabgab, antiquities officer and curator of the Famagusta Museum, whose life-long collection and beautiful garden made it one of the show places of the island. The neat little 'Theo' was charming and an authority on the history of Cyprus up to the present time. Since his death his sister lives alone on the property and although the long line of aloes gave form to the garden, the rest was overgrown and quite wild.

I looked at the large padlock. 'She's not here,' I said to the young U.N. officer who had brought me to the gate.

'Oh yes she is,' he said, producing a large key and putting it in the padlock. 'She arrives each morning from Famagusta for she sleeps at the hotel. If there has been any trouble or incidents, we keep this locked,' he added.

We walked up the avenue between the silver-grey thongs that shone in the sunlight like giant swords. Ahead stood the house, closed and shuttered and to the left was a smaller building that had been the servants' quarters in the old days.

'She is probably in there,' said the young man nodding towards it, 'it is cosier than the big house.'

At this moment a large hunting dog bounded out of the door and sprang at us until he recognized the uniform. A tiny dark woman with quick intelligent eyes came out of the door.

'Columbus!' she called. She was pleased to see us and so was the dog who jumped up at me. 'Columbus!'

'It's a good name,' I said.

'Yes, we called him that because as a puppy he was always exploring. Come into the house,' and she led the way across the court to the larger building.

The low bungalow-type house was deceptive for we entered a large hall that had a great air of spaciousness. It opened on to a series of equally big rooms where some good furniture, sculpture and ornaments, the remains of Theo's collection, could just be seen in the gloom. Miss Mogabgab ran ahead opening the shutters and letting in the daylight. We passed through into a well-proportioned oblong room that had a table running down the centre and with several old chairs. Here again, the shutters were opened.

'It's a lot of trouble for you,' I said.

'Oh no! It's fine to let the light in on all these things occasionally,' she said, glancing with pride at the objects around her.

The curtains were rich but faded into muted colours and the room had the waiting air of a place that had once been filled with life and people. Theo's presence still lingered and it was obvious, as we talked, how much his sister missed him.

We sipped some light Cyprus sherry which takes a little getting used to; and there was an air of picnicking in the dark house that had seen so many gatherings. It was an incongruous existence for our hostess who lived in a state of limbo, suspended between the hotel and this shuttered unused house.

When Theo bought large areas of the surrounding bare land and built his house, it was considered isolated and the land of no great value. Now, once the situation stabilizes, the whole area will become as valuable as the rest of Famagusta, and there had already been offers and plans afoot to develop it.

'In the meantime,' said Miss Mogabgab, 'I hold the fort

during the daytime; and Columbus takes over at night. It is an existence, hardly a life,' she added.

Later she came with us to the heavy gates and stood watching whilst the young soldier padlocked it once more. As we turned the car I looked back, the tiny black figure was making its way up the long avenue and Columbus bounded ahead.

I returned to the main road and a few miles farther on saw the ruins of Salamis to my right. Teucer founded the city on his return from the Trojan Wars and it remained an important centre for centuries. The ruins cover a vast area along the sea shore and not far away is a new hotel which would make the combined occupations of swimming and sight-seeing much more pleasant.

St Barnabas was born here and when he returned to the city with St Mark he was killed by the inhabitants. His companion found a rock tomb outside the city walls and buried him. Legend has it that in the fifth century the Archbishop Anthemios of Salamis had a vision in which he learned where the body lay, and when the grave was traced and opened, a manuscript of St Matthew's Gospel written by St Barnabas was found near the body. The Archbishop took the manuscript to the Emperor Zeno in Constantinople and related the whole story. This established the correct status of the Cypriot Church which became independent, and the Autocephalous Orthodox Church of Cyprus. From then on the Archbishops had the right to wear a cloak of imperial purple, to carry the imperial sceptre and to write their names in red ink – which they do to this day.

The grave of St Barnabas is on the other side of the present main road and a mausoleum has been built over it. It is a neat little edifice surrounded by a wrought-iron fence, and is a place of pilgrimage, for the waters in the cave tomb are believed to have miraculous healing qualities. I climbed down into the damp cavern where one candle was burning. It was still and the silence became a presence as it does in the desert. The thought of miracles did not seem extraordinary.

Out in the sunshine again I walked across to the Monastery of St Barnabas. It is a solid square building and attached to one side is a fifteenth-century church with two large domes. A group of high, straggling eucalyptus trees grew near a makeshift café, which was being painted in preparation for visitors.

In the main building a high arch led towards an inner courtyard, laid out as a garden, and surrounded by cells for the monks and novices. Two old monks with white beards came through a side door towards me. They are two of three blood brothers who have lived in the monastery since 1917, and as well as their ordinary duties they paint – and sell – highly colourful icons. In black robes and with their long white beards they were immensely picturesque. We went into a large room which was used as a studio. Easels, paints and some half finished icons stood near the window and it gave a cheerful industrious air to the otherwise sleepy scene. On one wall was a photograph of their mother whose stern eyes followed us round the room and this accentuated the air of domesticity. It was as though the monastery belonged entirely to the old monks who ran it as a going concern. Twelve years ago they built a bell tower for the church with their own money.

The monastery, church and the straggling eucalyptus trees make a definite landmark for the country is very flat here. It is the eastern end of the Mesaoria Plain, which lies between the Kyrenia Range and the Troodos Mountains.

I was driving towards the Kyrenia Range which spread along the horizon to the north, and within five miles I came to Trikome the birthplace of General Grivas who has had a long military career in both World Wars and Greece and has continued as leader of the guerrilla operations of EOKA. The actual house has been pulled down and a modern bungalow built in its place; the Cypriot, whose island could be described as one great archaeological 'dig', is not sentimental about more recent heroes and their birthplaces.

In the centre of an open square there is a beautiful little fifteenth-century Chapel of St James. This perfect example of Byzantine architecture pleased the late Queen Marie of Romania so much that she had an exact replica built at her home on the shores of the Black Sea.

The Land-Rover was climbing steadily towards the range, now fiery in the setting sun. The steep terraced slopes were patterned with newly planted trees and from the top the view was magnificent. Below lay the vast Mesaoria Plain with the wide sweep of Famagusta Bay in the distance, and behind me to the north, through gaps in the mountain peaks, there were glimpses across the water of the shores of Turkey. The hills around became deep bronze as the last shafts of sunlight picked up the small trees; and then the sun dropped out of sight with the suddenness common in these parts. One by one lights appeared on the plain below and gradually Famagusta and the grand curve of its bay were illuminated by a million specks of light.

I stopped at a five-road junction. The signposts were useless, for one was in Greek and the others pointed in a haphazard direction. Was it part of the Turkish invasion scare, or was I in a prohibited area? I took the most northerly road which was wet and sticky from a heavy downpour. The Land-Rover skidded round hair-pin bends, but in the enveloping blackness it was impossible to see what lay on each side. The mountain was completely deserted. I could wander round these hills all night. Perhaps it would be wiser to stop and camp. At this moment a dim light showed ahead and as I drew near two boys in uniform came towards the car. I had no way of knowing if they were Turkish or Greek.

'Where,' I asked the silent scrutinizing faces, 'is the nearest hotel?'

'Hotel' being a universal word dubbed me a tourist and the tension relaxed as in broken English they said there was an hotel at Kantara village three miles ahead.

'You will, however, not find a bed,' my informant continued.

'And what about Davlos?' I said, on the spur of the moment, although from what inner recesses of the mind this name had suddenly been conjured up, I did not know.

They nodded. 'Turn left at Kantara village, and after three miles you will find Davlos and Toni's Hotel down by the sea.'

They were Greek Cypriot soldiers and decided to escort me as far as Kantara to put me on the right track, which was just as well for at Kantara there were roads going in every direction.

The village lies about three miles from the castle of the same name and there was little else but the small bungalow café–

hotel and some empty holiday houses. The road descended in a series of hairpin bends along the northern slopes of the mountain range. Finally I clattered through the dark village of Davlos and along a straight road that led directly to the seashore where, tucked in a crescent cove, stood Toni's Hotel. It was in darkness except for one dim light on the top floor. Since the recent emergency there was a self-imposed blackout and anyone who could move from the north coast had done so. Certainly no tourists could be found in such a place. A head appeared at the lighted window and soon the electricity plant was turned on and the hotel came to life.

Toni had been to England where he had made enough money to return and build the hotel. Then he died suddenly leaving a widow and a young daughter who was married to the local schoolteacher. His daughter, Maria, was running the hotel with the help of her mother and her husband in the evenings. It was a large oblong building and each bedroom had a shower-bathroom and a balcony overlooking the cove. In the morning a varied assortment of peasants with their children on donkeys passed along the shore on their way to the fields beyond.

Davlos straggles along the buff of a hill that slopes from the range towards the sea. Many of the houses are empty and falling into disrepair for a number of the younger generation have emigrated to England or Australia. It is not yet contaminated by outsiders and still has that fine intangible quality of being 'undiscovered.'

'Now the coast road from Kyrenia has been opened up,' said Maria, 'and we will have many more people coming to the village.' She was bright and very go-ahead and hoped to make a success of the running of the hotel, despite the added work and responsibility of two small children. 'Look,' she continued, pointing to a small building down on the shingle beach, 'it is a hot spring which will cure your rheumatism. Isn't that a grand thing?'

I had to admit that it was.

Beyond the headland to the east are traces of a harbour and a pier with the ruins of an extensive ancient town. This, the great traveller Strabo believed, was the site of Aphrodisium: '. . . from Aphrodisium where the island is narrow,' he said, 'the journey to Salamis is seventy stadia,' which was the journey I had just made.

I made a day's excursion along the coast to Kyrenia, which is known as the Englishman's paradise with its picturesque harbour and beautiful Crusader Castle. Most of the British have braved it out and I saw two of them, peppery old boys, whose dogs were getting entangled in the panic precautions of barbed wire.

'What does Makarios think he's doing?' one of them said, 'Where in God's name does he think we're going to walk our dogs?'

The old Dome Hotel looked outraged and was almost empty. I lunched off turkey and plum pudding in splendid solitude. The emptiness had a slight air of jitters, despite the fact that this was certainly not the full tourist season, and perhaps it was because this is scheduled as the number one invasion area with the Dome as Turkish headquarters!

Afterwards I drove up to the Abbey of Bellapaise and couldn't have seen it at a better time for when the tourists return it will be very different. A developer is buying up many of the places and turning them into apartments, but the Abbey is still beautiful and merges into the scenery in an odd way I now remembered. I climbed farther to Lawrence Durrell's old place, the buying and repairing of which he describes so well in *Bitter Lemons*. It is sold now but is still pointed out as one of the village's attractions.

For old times' sake I had coffee under the Tree of Idleness in the village square and an old man warned me of its effect. 'You go on sitting there,' he said, 'and you'll always be lazy.' He was mentioned in Durrell's book and so he has become another bit of local colour.

There were few vehicles around, and on the plain I gave a lift to a priest who seemed surprised but very grateful. Perhaps they are considered unlucky in private life here as they are in Greece. As the plain rose into the hills we passed men with guns who were shooting rock doves, and when Davlos came into sight it was white and dark green against the soft blue hills, whilst beyond Kantara Castle formed a buttress at the end of the range.

2

First Steps

The direct route from Davlos to Nicosia, I was assured, necessitated retracing my steps over the Kyrenia Range and keeping to the Famagusta road until a right-hand turn brought me on to the main Nicosia road. It would have been possible to go along the coast to Kyrenia and turn south across the St Hilarion Pass; but this ran through the Turkish area from the pass to Nicosia, and no Greek Cypriot refers to these enclaves unless absolutely necessary.

Toni's family saw me off. I was armed with a huge jar of mountain honey, and was given many assurances that should I return, a desk would be found for me to write, and a gas heater against the cold. I climbed into the hills and the whole coastal plain spread each side of me. The shore wavered into small inlets and coves, and the mountains running down in slopes towards the shore made colour patterns of different density. We climbed over the range and here the mountain and the Mesaoria beyond had lost their golden sunset look but they were less ominous in the clear morning light – too peaceful to cause much trouble, and I wondered just what lay in store for me in the island's capital.

Nicosia had spread out on to the plain since my last visit. There were factories and large commercial garages and all the things that make a city ugly. The road led directly to the Famagusta Gate and the Turkish quarter, and for this reason the main flow of traffic has been re-directed to the left and runs along a wide avenue outside the city walls. It skirts the dry moat which is now a series of gardens and playing fields. The solid ramparts form a perfect circle of three miles, although from Constantine the Great's time until 1567 the city had a circumference of nine miles. Then the Venetians reduced the size to make the city more compact and easier to defend, they rounded it off with bastions and gates and completely levelled the ground outside, destroying everything, including fine buildings, in the process.

I kept to the walls, for the Ledra Palace Hotel was situated beyond them towards the Kyrenia Gate, and eventually I must come to it. Suddenly ahead was a road block with barbed wire, oil drums, and a U.N. Observation Post. As I drew up a Cyprus police officer appeared. The hotel, he informed me, lay in the no-man's land between the Greek and the Turkish sector!

'Is it still an hotel?' I asked. He was an incredibly handsome young man, olive-skinned and unaware of his attraction – a young Laurence Olivier.

He nodded but hesitated.

'I'm from England,' I added – which could have been good or bad, according to his politics.

'Go right on ahead,' he said, 'first on the left,' and waved me on.

The hotel was unchanged except that another storey had been added. Most of one floor was taken over by the U.N. personnel, the sand-bags and oil drums surrounded the ball-room entrance. Just beyond, where the road led to the Turkish quarter and the Kyrenia Gate, the 'border' was blocked by a series of zig-zag drums and barriers. The hotel has been the main one in Nicosia for a decade or two and is known to every journalist visiting the Middle East. Now there are several other first-class hotels but the Ledra still collects most of the personalities, businessmen, and journalists as well as the tourists. Despite its first-class rating and size it still has the old personal service and friendliness, and 'Pan' the head porter is quite indispensable.

In the bar overlooking the garden, the waiter – a man whose plumpness made him appear older than he was – greeted me cheerily. He had been the enthusiastic little bell-hop of my earlier visit!

Nicosia, like all cities in transition, is an uneasy place; it has lost its original character and hasn't yet established a new one. The fact that it is cut in half by the Turkish and Greek Quarters, doesn't help matters. The north part of the city where many of the old buildings and cathedrals are, is now Turkish. Their territory spreads out to the north along the Kyrenia Range and it makes their largest enclave. The southern part of the old city and far beyond the walls has become the Nicosia of the Greek Cypriots. In this area is Maximos Square, the Piccadilly Circus of Greek Nicosia and from here I crossed the causeway leading to the notorious Ledra Street which was the scene of so many riots and murders during the EOKA uprisings. The narrow street looked innocent enough now and its whole length was lined with small shops of every kind. Crowds dodged in and out of the heavy traffic which moved at snail's pace. At the far end of the street the crowd began to thin out and at a sign marked WARNING GREEN LINE it stopped completely. The road beyond led to the no-man's land between the two sectors and it was eerie walking beyond this spot and along the empty connecting street, for the bombed, barracked and sandbagged buildings were completely unoccupied. Except for the occasional U.N. soldier there was no sign of life, although an odd sense of watchfulness hung over the deserted street.

The Archbishop's Palace and some of the administration buildings still lie inside the walls on the Greek side, but beyond, new buildings are springing up amongst the solid stone structures of the British era, which are still used by various Government Departments. A series of low barrack-like buildings house the Ministry of Information where Mr. Christoulodou, the Minister, welcomed me, gave me a magnificent illustrated book on Cyprus and handed me on to his second-in-command, Peter Stylianakis. Peter was quiet and sensible and had none of the exhibitionism of some P.R.O.s.

Cities and the European colony in such places have a nullifying effect on me. Not being a tenacious journalist I can't penetrate the layer of sophistication right away to find the people and the facts below. I must start from the other end, in outlying places, from where the city dweller probably came. Then later he will be more understandable and recognizable beneath the gloss.

Many countries when they have gained independence from the British suffer, for competent men are not always given the responsible jobs, perhaps because they were previously singled out by the British. It was going to take some time to work out the political situation; the strange combination of Western diplomacy and Eastern intrigue, and the heartbreaking tangle of the Greek–Turkish Cypriot question.

It was obvious that journalists and tourists saw little of the 'other' side, nor were they encouraged to do so, and most of them left the island with a very slanted picture. True there were trouble spots where permission to visit was necessary from the U.N. Commander, or Turkish enclaves whose own leader might not encourage visitors and certainly no Greek Cypriot vehicle would enter such a place at the moment. Now, because of the recent emergency the embargoes were likely to be more stringent. I was lucky in having my own transport and a lone female can often pass barriers that would remain closed to more official-looking bodies. However, it was contemporary and unbiased knowledge of the whole scene that was missing. Peter came to my rescue.

'There is an Englishwoman staying at the Ledra,' he said, 'she's been coming here many years. She is a writer. Very intelligent,' he added.

I found her reading the latest U.N. report in the lounge. She was tall with a well-shaped English face, natural light-coloured hair that framed a fine forehead; and a direct look. Peter was right, she had one of those clear concise minds that I envy very much. Her arrival, just at the time of the recent emergency was providential for, if anyone could sort out the causes and undercurrents, it was Nancy Crawshaw. I soon found that she shared my dislike of the customary Christmas festivities that lay ahead. When the time came we would go to Paphos and Aphrodite country, for I had the transport and she had the brains – an ideal combination.

In the press office of U.N. headquarters in Nicosia the Colonel in charge promised to signal ahead to the commanding officer of the British contingent stationed in Paphos, just before we intended to go.

The island is divided into seven districts or zones and each zone is manned by a different contingent i.e. the Swedes were at the moment controlling the Famagusta Zone and the British the Paphos area. Each contingent has its own headquarters with posts at strategical positions. Many of the different countries' soldiers are volunteers but the British have no option and are drafted from the army. As soldiers their position seems frightful, for they are not allowed to use arms except in extreme circumstances of self-defence and yet they act as a buffer between the two sides, in order to prevent a conflict being exaggerated. It says something for the common-sense of all concerned that in this present impasse, where there was no Government as set down by the Constitution – for it was broken by the conflict – the U.N. Force was able to move in and function with the consent of both Greek and Turkish Cypriots. This happened as far back as the spring of 1964 when the United Nations Peace Keeping Force – UNFICYP – took over its duties in Cyprus. It was the outcome of the crisis of the preceding Christmas which had thrown the island into chaos, and a British force was brought in from the Sovereign Base to keep the peace. A series of negotiations followed and finally an agreement was made and UNFICYP moved in to take over the job.

Within a month of their arrival on the island, UNFICYP had their first taste of the problems and situations that they were to encounter up to the present day. The Turkish Cypriots took and held the castle of St Hilarion which gave them control of the Kyrenia–Nicosia road and the centre ridges of the Kyrenia Range. The Greeks attacked the castle hoping to drive the Turks out, when the U.N. Forces intervened and arranged a 'cease-fire' between the two sides. UNFICYP then established a post near by, thus making a buffer between the two sides, and similar posts were set up at other trouble spots, such as Paphos, Artemis Avenue in Larnaca, Kokkina on the north-west coast. Any Greek Cypriot wishing to visit Kyrenia from Nicosia must either make a long detour around the Turkish enclave, or go with the U.N. convoy which leaves each morning and evening. But tension is never far below the surface and minor incidents happen from time to time. Others blow up into larger ones, as the recent Ayios Theodoros-Kophinou incident had done.

Whilst the Turkish Cypriots depended more or less on Turkey, and used the threat of Turkish invasion as their trump card, the present stalemate has not affected the Greek Cypriots overmuch, for the running of the island is in their hands. However, they must realize that no solution that would be acceptable to the outside world can come about unless the island is morally independent of Greece. But Enosis – union with Greece – has been the slogan for so long that it will take very drastic measures to break it down – economically, politically and morally advisable as it might be. Also over the last few years the Greek Governments, have not after all, had great stability. The majority of the Turkish Cypriots, shattered by the troubles, want partition, when each side has a separate part of the island and each governs itself. This would probably be economically disastrous for them and the island, and both sides would grow even farther apart. In the meantime their position does not improve as they still lead a separate existence in a semi-state of siege, depending in some degree on aid from Turkey and the political whims of their Greek brothers.

It is possible to shut your eyes to the whole situation as many tourists do, for otherwise the Greek–Turkish situation is quite unreal. I would leave the Ledra Palace Hotel and turn right to the Greek sector, or left to the Turkish enclave; smiling at Greek soldiers or at the Turkish ones. Crossing the no-man's-land towards the Turkish enclave I was observed by U.N. soldiers, the Greeks and the Turks as well; and ahead was a barricade of earth-filled oil drums that zig-zagged across the road. Behind them was a small Turkish sentry box and friendly Turkish policemen. The area beyond the barricades ran through streets of bungalows towards the administration centre. There was a lack of maintenance everywhere and the streets were practically traffic free as petrol was still rationed severely. The large bare Sarayi Hotel was in need of paint but Rustems was still the best bookshop in this part of the world. I felt that *nothing* would stop its owner from ordering the books for his shop whether he sold them or not. The few restaurants that were open served excellent meals at half the price of the 'other side'. The old hall where I had watched, mesmerized, the whirling Dervishes years ago, was a museum now although the narrow gallery of tombs beyond the hall was still there and with the odd 'happy' feeling I never could quite fathom. Near-by is a frightening little Museum of Horror which has relics and photographs of the recent atrocities.

It was a stroke of luck, in view of the recent troubles, that I had brought my own vehicle, for the British registration number made it possible for me to go anywhere and into all the enclaves. I was already recognized at the various borders and it was not necessary to join the convoy of Greek cars that left each morning to pass through the Turkish enclave on their way to Kyrenia. These vehicles were escorted by UNFICYP and they returned each evening. They set off at high speed, the UNFICYP vehicles fore and aft, with lights flashing, and it was necessary when alone, to stop and let them pass.

Along the road were several sign boards erected by the Turks, with propaganda for their cause; the most poignant simply stated: 'ISLAND WITHOUT SEA'.

3

The Tale of Two Villages

Tragedy is even more shattering in brilliant sunlight, the contrast is too great and it is a stark reminder that there are better things to do with life. On the southern slopes of the island thirty miles from Nicosia are the villages of Ayios Theodoros and Kophinou. The houses and buildings of the latter were blasted and charred, old women still whimpered with shock; and the damage to the mosque's minaret looked equally obscene.

Before we left for Paphos, Nancy and I decided to see for ourselves the battleground of the flare-up of the previous month which had drastically affected the chances of settling the Cyprus dispute. Reports on the whole situation were contradictory, to say the least.

'We might not be able to see anything,' she said.

'Well, we can try.'

We set off along the main Nicosia to Limassol road which runs through the Turkish village of Kophinou and three miles beyond at Skarinou Bridge a turning to the left leads to the mixed Greek–Turkish village of Ayios Theodoros.

The situation before the flare-up was similar to that in many mixed villages where trouble is averted with the help of the U.N. Peace Keeping Force; the difference in this case being the presence and action of so many of the National Guard who were on the spot and the whole affair was a culmination of rising tension on both sides. The September summit talks had failed and there were repeated speeches by Greek Cypriots in favour of Enosis, which was far from diplomatic at a time when relations were at their very worst. To top it all a month previously Denktash, the President of the Turkish Cypriot Communal Chamber, who had been exiled for four years by the Greek Cypriot Government for his part in the 1963 troubles, landed secretly in the Karpas where he was arrested. Immediately there was anxiety for his safety and the U.N. urged his

Outside a school in Paphos, 'Cypriot boy killing British lion'

The church of Chryssopolitissa, Paphos

release. During his detention the President of the Greek Cypriot House of Representatives, Glavkos Clerides, visited him. The two men, both barristers, had been friends and the talk was the first of many that have helped matters between the two sides. But Denktash's appearance and arrest at this moment merely added to the tension. (It is to the Greek's credit that he was later released and sent back to Turkey without any charge being made against him.)

The trouble started at Ayios Theodoros, the small village we were making for. The road from Skarinou Bridge runs through the Turkish sector first and the Greek Cypriot police from Skarinou passed along it to reach the Greek sector. This arrangement worked reasonably well until there were shooting incidents and reprisals along the main highway near by. The Greek Cypriot police decided not to use the road until the tension caused by these incidents lessened. They therefore made a detour and came to their own Greek sector of the village from the south. Some time later however they decided to re-establish their right to use the north road again. The Turks would not agree and the Greeks became impatient, determined now to exert their authority and right to use the road. The U.N. tried to mediate for it was felt that any patrols by the Greeks would, at this stage, merely incite the Turks. But on the day UNFICYP informed the Greeks that the Turks were ready to agree to the opening of the road, two patrols, with an escort of National Guards, started along the north road; and these were followed by another the next morning.

President Makarios, General Grivas and the Minister of the Interior had held a conference, but whether they decided to go ahead with the patrols immediately, or General Grivas took matters into his own hands, has never been established. Although the three patrols had continued without interference, the Turkish Cypriots now sent a warning that any further patrols would meet with resistance. Despite this, a fourth one set out and this time they found a tractor and a plough drawn across their path; almost immediately some Greek armoured cars arrived from the south and as the soldiers were clearing the road, firing broke out. The National Guard and the Cyprus police opened fire and this was the signal for firing to start all over the village. It was no mere skirmish for as well as small arms, heavy machine guns and armoured cars with two-pounder guns were used and later even medium mortars and artillery weapons were brought into action.

At almost the same time armoured cars and infantry moved in against the Turkish Cypriot positions above the village of Kophinou and the National Guard took up a stand alongside some of the posts of the local U.N. contingent, the 1st Battalion the Royal Green Jackets. This brought the Green Jackets under fire also and for the next few hours the riflemen on duty (whose task it is to observe and report the fighting) were in dangerously exposed positions between the two sides. On one post they lost contact with their headquarters when their radio was struck by a bullet and here also mortar bombs fell a few yards from their position. It was after this incident that three weapons were taken from the U.N. post by the National Guard.

The contingent's headquarters came under fire for nearly two hours, but it is the U.N. soldiers' job in such a situation to stay where they are and report accurately throughout the battle, which the boys did.

The Government of Turkey immediately saw it as a planned attack by General Grivas who was using weapons beyond those needed for such an undertaking. A stiff message was sent, making it plain that if the National Guard and the Cypriot police did not leave the Turkish Cypriot areas of both villages, Turkey would take immediate action. Despite this warning, the Greek police insisted on sending another patrol along the road, to assert their authority.

Now the Turkish population on the mainland was demanding war and their Government was authorized to mobilize troops. It seemed that Turkey, once roused, had decided to settle the Cyprus question once and for all. There was panic in Cyprus and the U.N. Security Council called an emergency meeting at the request of the Cyprus Government. A Turkish landing became a possibility and trenches and air-raid shelters were dug. Turkish warships were sighted off the north coast, and planes flew low over the coastal plain; it took just six minutes for them to arrive from Turkey. Some Britishers and foreign residents moved to the British Sovereign Base at Dhekelia;

tourists left overnight and a large group who arrived at Nicosia airport on a package tour, were promptly sent back again.

On the following morning the Greek Government ordered General Grivas to withdraw his troops and a ceasefire was finally arranged for 16th November. Despite this, mopping-up operations continued which accounted for more deaths. Turkey insisted on the permanent removal of General Grivas, and the expulsion of all illegal troops from the island.

When the clearing up began it was found that there were twenty-five Turkish civilians dead including some women and many people were severely wounded. The Greek Cypriots suffered only two or three casualties. In Kophinou almost every building received damage of some kind.

The reason for the large attack remains a mystery, for to run several patrols at short intervals was obviously done to incite the Turkish Cypriots. Did the Greek Cypriots want a large-scale war that could so easily have followed? Were they testing Turkey's reactions? Or were they seriously concerned that the Turks were trying to enlarge and consolidate a south coast enclave? Perhaps after all it was the natural outcome of having so many Greek and Turkish troops on the island whose numbers had swelled far above the agreed figure. If any good came out of the tragedy it was that these extra troops were sent back to their own countries; and not before the ordinary islander had become extremely tired of having foreign troops around, no matter which side they were on.

Nancy, who had most of the island's contemporary history at her fingertips, would make more sense of it than most, and we decided to go direct to Ayios Theodoros, the source of the trouble. The turn-off at Skarinou Bridge ran along the edge of the river Pendaskino and the road climbed to a slight rise where there was a deserted school house, and Ayios Theodoros lay along the opposite bank. It was here that the tractor and plough had blocked the road. We stopped, trying to reconstruct the scene in our minds as a Land-Rover appeared, coming quickly towards us on the narrow way. The vehicle swerved and pulled up with a jerk. Two husky men looked in at my Land-Rover; 'Dames!' their faces clearly registered. They were Australian U.N. police, stationed at Ayios Theodoros.

'Can we go through?' I asked. The darker one nodded and eyed me intently. 'Yes,' I said, 'I'm Australian!'

After a good fifteen minutes of the relative merits of Sydney and Melbourne we started to move off.

'There's no road block or anything?'

'No. Just the "Brits" over the bridge, but you go right ahead. 'Bye, sorry we can't show you round, but we've to be in H.Q. by noon.'

The road ran down to the river, and across the bridge there were some British soldiers sitting on a terrace.

'Better not stop,' I suggested, 'otherwise they may have to hold us up, whether they want to or not.'

The village extended each side along the river which was very low now and a good watering place for donkeys. Olive and fruit trees grew on the hill beyond and it looked sleepy and quiet; incapable of the tensions and fighting that had gone on so recently. We crossed the bridge and drove through a narrow street of low houses. At the first cross roads we turned right towards the Turkish quarter and bumped over the rough surface. The mud and stone huts were set on rising ground and there were few people about. No children at all.

'There's a café,' said Nancy, pointing to an open barn-like structure.

We left the Land-Rover and crossed to the café which had a low counter, a few tables and dozens of chairs. There were four elderly men sitting near the opening and another behind the counter. We asked for a drink to establish our nationality.

One of the men put a couple of chairs for us. 'Please have something, whatever you like.'

By the time we had been given glasses of fresh lemon juice, the café was almost full, for word had gone around. They were nearly all elderly men, and quite friendly. When they discovered I was Australian the atmosphere eased considerably for the Australian police were very popular amongst them. We tried to draw them out about the recent troubles but their knowledge of English suddenly deserted them!

We rose to go. 'How much do we owe?' I asked.

The elderly man shook his head and the whole company murmured dissent. 'It's a pleasure,' he said.

We thanked them and moved out into the sunshine again. 'I really think we should have paid,' I said.

'Let us, at *least*, do that.' I turned, a young man had followed us out. 'Come and see us again,' he added, 'we like visitors. It's very quiet here – *now*.' And he gave me a wry smile.

The Greek sector was quiet also but its buildings were far more substantial. The ugly nineteenth-century church of St Theodore was undergoing extensive repairs. We climbed to the hill beyond and looked down on the long stretch of the village and if there were scars, they had already been hidden. It was difficult to associate the quiet sunny village with the troubles that had recently made headline news all over the world.

Kophinou was another thing. As we drove off the main road into the village it was obvious it had received much worse treatment. There were burnt houses and others had bomb holes or were spattered with shrapnel. The Turkish police officer was surprised to see us for few people came to look for themselves. The officer was still stunned and shocked by the course of events and very willing to give us an escort.

'They even damaged the minaret of the mosque,' he said.

A young man took us through the muddy streets, we saw a few people but there was no traffic at all. As we walked our companion talked of the day of the attack which had come so suddenly. The women and children, and all who could, took shelter in the mosque.

'Look!' he pointed to the damaged minaret which hung at an odd angle, with part of its decoration swinging loose. 'They were *silly* to do that.'

In a narrow street he opened a heavy charred door that led into an inner court. A middle-aged woman came towards us, crying miserably. Around the door was more charred wood. Her husband had been a coloured man, a large cheerful person who was liked in the village and when she went to the mosque he stayed behind to look after their house. She said the Greek soldiers came and opened the door, throwing a grenade or petrol in, and setting it alight. The husband was burnt to death. She cried plaintively pointing at the charred wood.

We walked on through the mud, and eucalyptus trees made

speckled shade around us. A small room opened directly on to the street, its door and ceiling had gone and there was nothing inside but the remains of an iron bedstead which took up most of the room. An old man, too old to move, lived here and he had been burnt in his bed. Farther on there were broken windows and spattered walls, the familiar marks of war, and through the eucalyptus trees we could see the hill of upper Kophinou across the main road, from where we were a perfect target.

'Twenty-five killed,' said our friend, suddenly.

'It is all so useless. . . .'

The young man nodded. 'Useless,' he repeated, 'but we will kill if we have to – *and* brutally, I have no illusions about that – but not in this dirty way.'

4

Paphos Bound

There is no relationship so fraught with danger, so sensitive to disaster, as that of travelling companions. It is a much more subtle association than most people think, and yet they will team up with as little thought as they give a whirlwind courtship – and often with just as disastrous results.

What makes a good travelling combination and what characteristics ensure that you will travel peacefully together? It is certainly not easy to tell, and the results are often unexpected. I have travelled for the first time with a friend and almost wrecked a friendship of many years' standing, whilst a complete stranger with whom I apparently have little in common fits in and becomes part of my travelling world right away. As well as a certain willingness to adapt – which anyhow is the first prerequisite of the traveller – similar habits in eating and sleeping rate much higher than you would think. Nancy is not only intelligent, which is always satisfying, but she has a lot of common sense and likes, as I do, to eat simply *en route*, and have a good meal at night.

For those in a hurry, Paphos can be reached from Nicosia in three hours. The main roads are quite good, although in some places the edges are breaking which makes them a little too narrow. Also, Cypriots drive with a certain abandon and this has to be watched.

It was sunny and clear as we ran south, skirting widely the Troodos Massif. Finally, to our left we saw the famous Stavrovouni Monastery perched on its bare mountain, 5,000 feet above us. Such is its height and isolation, that for centuries ships used it as a landmark-lighthouse from many miles out to sea.

As we neared the village of Kophinou the U.N. troops were still very much in evidence. The sunny little village with its war scars lay below. There were ladders propped up against some of the walls and the business of reconstruction had begun.

We felt a sense of relief when we finally came to the coast.

There had been so many conflicting opinions about our travelling around at this particular time. The sea seemed neutral – and we could both swim!

Right on the water's edge there is a solid wall which is pounded by the sea and in the water below there are traces of buildings and mosaics. Other ruins lay on the opposite side of the road and this is all that is left of Amathus, one of the most ancient cities on the island and capital of one of the Nine Kingdoms. Richard Coeur de Lion captured the city and destroyed it during his attack on the island. It was also the centre of the copper-mining industry that now functions in other parts of the island.

Four miles farther on we took the by-pass round the port of Limassol, which is being industrialized beyond the capacity of its narrow winding streets. The by-pass has ceased to be one and has become a busy shopping centre that caters mainly for the British from the Sovereign Base area four miles farther along the coast.

There are no signposts or barriers marking the entrance to the area, but the sudden appearance of well-kept streets, orderly houses and the vivid green playing fields, make it easily recognizable.

During the time the British were in Cyprus they built two large military bases on the south coast, one at Dhekelia south of Famagusta and this one at Akrotiri which lies just west of Limassol. The bases remained British under the terms of the Cyprus Constitution after the island was given independence, although Archbishop Makarios managed to have the size reduced and to increase British financial aid.

Dhekelia is being slowly 'run down' but Akrotiri remains the headquarters of the Army and Air Force in the Middle East. It is a small well-run centre with administration buildings, barracks, suburbs, shopping areas and an airfield. On the far cliff beyond the playing fields is the exclusive residential area for the commanding officers, the Air Vice Marshal and the Commander-in-Chief, Major General David Lloyd Owen. The latter's exploits during World War II, especially with the Long Range Desert Group in North Africa, make him one of my special heroes.

The road was no Corniche, but it roughly skirted the coast and there were many glimpses of coves and beaches. Inland the ground rose slowly towards the Troodos Mountains and the slopes were covered with vineyards. On the hills and in the valleys we caught sight of little villages, and we passed through others that seemed untouched by time, except for the ribbon of road that ran through them.

We came suddenly on the huge rocks of Petra tou Romiou. They stand at the point of a tiny inlet and it was here, so they say, that Aphrodite rose from the foam. At certain times of the year, with unfailing regularity, foam does whirl round the great rocks. Some odd magic hangs over the place, which even the picnic parties who come to bathe and laze on the rocky shore cannot entirely dispel. Nancy, who is a bathing addict, had a quick dip, but I – coming from warmer climes – found it much too cold.

From now on we were in Aphrodite country and every few miles there was some reminder of the goddess. Not that her influence isn't felt in the rest of the island for if one searches there are the remains of her temples everywhere and a number of the monasteries have been built on their foundations. The legend of Aphrodite and her various places of worship has become a symbol for the tourist trade and it is in danger of being as overdone here, as the Queen of Sheba is in Ethiopia.

The worship of women, it would seem, is inherent in the island where love and lovers come into their own. There was the goddess of Fertility, and then the arrival of Aphrodite, who was an immediate success, for in no time at all there were temples and sanctuaries dedicated to her all over the island. The Romans renamed her Venus. And the Christians? They are always conservative about lionizing women. The Virgin Mary perhaps took her place, leaving Aphrodite a kind of overall patron saint of the island.

Each spring she mourns the death of Adonis killed by a jealous boar, and it is her feet, bleeding from the thorns as she ran to her wounded lover, that dyed the small wild rose pink. And now in the spring she calls them again to bloom, together with the deeper-toned anemone that is the blood of Adonis. Nowhere else in the world is spring such a joyous time of re-birth.

Less than six miles from Petra tou Rominou we came to the ruins of Palea or old Paphos where the most famous of all Aphrodite's temples stood. In the spring a great pilgrimage took place and people arrived from all over the island; and ships brought them to Nea or New Paphos ten miles to the west. The long road from the sea to the Temple here was scented by trees and shrubs that grew along the route. Each year the pilgrims returned to celebrate in different ways according to their particular stage of initiation, and after a series of contests and dancing, singing and feasting, a procession made its way to the sea, which was honoured as the birthplace of the Goddess. As a final ceremony the maidens of the crowd gathered on the shore wearing white robes and garlands of fresh flowers in their hair, to sacrifice their virginity as an offering to Aphrodite. It is small wonder that the Temple became famous far beyond the island's shores. The Christians put a stop to all this, but the islander today enjoys himself nevertheless, and the present festivities and celebrations have echoes of the early Temple Rites. The Whitsun Pentecost or Kataklymos takes place by the shore where after dancing and contests of all kinds, everyone goes out to the sea in small boats for the splashing contest, a survival of the old rights.

We pulled up outside a long Lusignan structure which is the only building still standing. It is used as a rather disorganized but pleasant museum with a few statues and pieces of carving propped up against the walls. Outside we wandered through the many ruins, tracing earlier buildings, the wide open courts, with steps leading to the main hall and saw many chambers each just big enough to take one pilgrim, and there were gateways through which the pilgrims arrived from the east and the west.

Many fallen white columns had been replaced in part and we tried to visualize the city when it was the island's capital in the fourth century B.C. It was here that King Pygmalion fell in love with the statue he had created and Aphrodite brought her to life for him and called her Galatia.

Kinyras, the high Priest-King of Aphrodite's shrine, and his successors continued to rule even when the city became just the religious centre. But when the Romans took possession of the island in 56 B.C. it lost its significance and earthquakes later brought the city to near ruin. In the next century the Byzantine Emperor Theodorius banned worship in pagan temples and Aphrodite's famous temple ceased to exist. Perhaps it was the pleasant situation and the vast amount of finely cut stone that prompted the Lusignans to build their royal pavilion *La Covocle* here. It gave the place a certain importance for the time being, but the Saracen raids of the fourteenth and fifteenth centuries gradually reduced the city to its present state.

The small present-day village of Kouklia stands alongside the ruins. Its houses and streets have a cardboard-like quality in comparison with the other finely worked stone. Both Turks and Greeks live in the village and for this reason perhaps they regarded us sullenly.

On the last lap of our journey we passed through the small town of Yeroskipos, the Sacred Garden, and this was one of the main stopping places for the pilgrims from New Paphos. Somewhere near-by in the hills, perhaps traces of the Sacred Garden could be found. It is an expedition, a search that must sometime be undertaken.

It was already late afternoon when we came towards Ktima which is the name given to the modern town of Paphos. It stands two miles back from the sea-shore on a buff and the first thing that confronted us as we drove along the main street was a large relief plaque outside the secondary school depicting a Cypriot schoolboy killing the British lion. A fine welcome!

Peter had booked us into the New Olympus, the best hotel in the town where we had a room apiece and shared a bathroom. Part of the hotel was taken over by the Australian U.N. police as their headquarters; they were all very large, cheerful and extremely noisy. The town is known for its fine air which is another name for fierce winds that blow incessantly and particularly through cracks in our French windows.

Paphos is a small provincial town with a narrow main shopping street, a square with administration buildings and police station, and a series of well-to-do bungalows set in gardens. It is surrounded by rich agricultural country. At the far end of the main street shattered buildings form the division between Greek and Turkish quarters. The town has produced many Cypriots who are now in high positions both in politics and business; and a number of the plots and intrigues that have affected the island's history first saw the light of day here. I never could dispel an underlying air of intrigue, an odd feeling of hate.

Mr. George Iliades is a man of many parts in Paphos. He is a schoolmaster, an archaeologist and Hon. Curator of the little District Museum, as well as having a private museum of his own. He is dark-eyed with an aquiline nose, a lot of dignity and is completely absorbed in the town's history and the old treasures it is yielding up. The most spectacular treasure is the Roman villa near the harbour where some of the best mosaics in this part of the Mediterranean can be found. He took us immediately to the flat plain below the town which runs to the sea and is the site of the various cities of Paphos since Agapenor was wrecked offshore and founded the first one. Earthquakes have systematically destroyed the cities and the present ruins are Roman, for it was during this subsequent era that the town became the most important in the island. The rock-cut tombs below ground level have been used from the Late Bronze age up to the Christian era and we traced crosses carved in the rock. Nancy's whole concentration is on contemporary history whilst our friend's interest seemed to flag at anything later than A.D. 100. When two strong personalities meet – and differ – sparks fly. I concentrated on driving the Land-Rover and resolved to return later and 'do' the ruins at my leisure.

The Roman villa, however, brought a certain calm by virtue of the beauty of the mosaics. The villa stands slightly inland from the small harbour and was discovered by chance in 1962 when a plough upturned a piece of mosaic and the excavations were begun. The work revealed a large residence of twenty-two rooms and that an earthquake had razed most of the walls to near-ground level. The rooms are grouped round an open court and colonnade, and the fourteen mosaics are beautifully preserved. There are mythological subjects and hunting scenes as well as conventional patterns made up of ancient symbols. A large metal awning, which is ugly but practical, covers the whole area, and raised cat-walks have been built over the fallen walls between the rooms so that it is possible to see the mosaics at close range. We persuaded the custodian to throw water over the floors and the mosaics were suddenly revealed in their magnificent brilliant colours.

Who owned the villa? Nobody knows. But it was obviously a notable citizen or governor of the town. They know it was destroyed in the fourth century and during the excavations a large collection of coins dating from the reigns of Ptolemy V and Ptolemy XI were found near the skeleton of a slave who had been crushed by the debris. It took sixteen centuries for his crime to come to light.

On a deserted beach west of Paphos and near the village of Khlorakas is the picturesque barque *Aghios Georghios*. It has been beached here since early 1955 when during the EOKA troubles an attempt to land both men and arms for the rebels, was foiled by the British Naval Patrol. A priest who came from the village to show us the way lost two fingers in the fracas, for some of the locals had been involved in the operation.

Behind the barque on higher ground stands a small chapel. It was erected from funds donated by a local girl, Zena Gunther, who married a Texan millionaire. Now a widow, she has given a great amount of money to projects and churches all over the island.

Our hotel had a small bar, an unused sitting-room and a large dining-room with a fleet of large white tablecloths. The manager was a worried little man who didn't live in and was permanently admonishing the Australians to be quiet. The only other guests were a Scottish doctor and his wife.

If you are not staying in a five-star hotel which will be centrally heated, you can be as cold in Cyprus in December as anywhere else in the world. Little or no provision is made for the few months of cold; it is such a short time so why bother, is the Cypriot's reaction to complaints. We ganged up with the Scots and bullied the manager into producing logs for the fireplace in the dining-room and we sat around it gradually thawing.

Later that evening the District Officer, the doctor and a few leading citizens – all men – arrived to see us. They sat in a circle, giving out some very 'set' propaganda. Nancy listened for a while, and then with a couple of short but sharp facts and statistics, she arrested their eloquence in mid-air, so to speak. They left soon afterwards in surprised silence – and we didn't see them again.

The British U.N. contingent have their headquarters in a large private house on the edge of the town and the Company Commander, Major Evelegh, was prepared to be helpful. The British seem to take more interest in the people and the situation than most other nationalities; so they were able to bring Nancy up-to-date on the present local situation. One wonders if it was fair to have the British Tommy here in this capacity. Memories can't be all that short and the violence and murders of the EOKA period is not so long ago.

Major Evelegh agreed to escort us into the Turkish quarter of the town, which is completely cut off from the rest of the population. We had tried to find our way through the labyrinth of bombed houses and empty streets but with no success. Tension between the two sides has always been strong here, culminating in a bloody battle in 1964. Incidents continue with gloomy regularity but they are often sorted out with the help of the U.N. army and police before they get out of hand.

It is obvious that most visitors to Paphos who 'do' the ruins, marvel at the mosaics, eat good fish meals at the harbour restaurants and go swimming at Coral Bay, never meet a Turkish Cypriot. Even if they are interested in the island's recent troubles and history their inquiries are brushed aside with vague shrugs and assurances that the Turks are 'difficult', and there the matter stands. Understandable perhaps that they don't pursue things further, for tourists are on holiday and realities can wait until the holiday is over. A visit to a Turkish Cypriot enclave might not be their idea of a nice day's outing – rewarding and interesting as it may be.

It is always a shock to leave the busy crowded Greek section and come to the vein of derelict and smashed buildings between the two sides. Here in Paphos the devastation is worse than usual. There was a sudden quiet, a sense of watchfulness and the buildings appeared to close in on us along the narrow street. Who is to know that this might not be the exact moment for another flare-up – and there you would be in the no-man's-land between! Major Evelegh's Land-Rover swung out of sight ahead and as I drove round a sharp bend we spied a U.N. flag on top of a high building. From this high vantage point the soldiers commanded a good view of both sides. Ahead of us was the Turkish enclave and already a few people could be seen. Even before we came level with them we sensed the tempo of life had changed, the pace was slower.

We stopped in a small square which lay at a rakish angle on the side of the hill. Most of the buildings were tiny shops except for a two-storey one which was the Turkish Administration Headquarters. In a small café near by a few old men sat on long wooden benches, and one old automobile was parked in front of it. Another man stood in the doorway of a small shop on the other side of the square – there was nobody else.

A certain mystery surrounds the Turkish Cypriot leaders and attempts to meet and talk with them have a slight cloak and dagger atmosphere. They may be mainland Turks or someone unpopular with the Greek Cypriot administration. I wondered that they gave interviews at all. The leader wore dark glasses. He was plainly dressed in a grey suit, middle-aged, and a lawyer by profession. He seemed to be dealing personally with all the problems, large and small, of the enclave. As well as the political side there was acute lack of accommodation for refugees who had left villages no longer safe, and difficulties arose over supplies of food and building materials.

Leaving Nancy to fathom the intricate workings of the Turkish financial position, I went with Ali, one of the assistants, to look at the refugee quarters. He was a sensible young man, relaxed and easygoing. There is little they can do about the situation, but their acceptance of it and their innate good humour is very touching.

The refugees were housed in odd rooms, and on the hillside beyond was a shanty town of mud-brick and corrugated iron. The hill faces the sea, but none of the people in the enclave were allowed on the sea-front for it was patrolled by the Greeks.

There is an atmosphere common to all refugee camps, a sense of waiting; and of no interest in starting a new life. Is it the shock of disruption, or the passiveness of people no longer in control of their own destiny? Whatever it is, they all have the same inert dignity. In a narrow street, small store-rooms, open except for rough doors, had a family apiece living in them, and ten other families had shared a large barn for the past four years. It was spotlessly clean and iron beds were set head-to-toe along the walls. A few family possessions in boxes were pushed under the beds. During the recent emergency some people had moved into the slaughter-house, and two families who shared one room, took it in turns to have the place to sleep in.

'It isn't much to ask,' said Ali quietly, as we climbed into an old Opel car, 'to be allowed to live as human beings.'

The car spluttered its way out to a rocky rise which was as near the sea as they were allowed to go. The car's brakes had to be pumped a long time before we finally came to a stop in front of a café. The small structure had been built by the entire community and iron rods protruded from the flat roof for, as Ali said, 'we shall build another floor later on.'

A young man greeted us enthusiastically for I was their first outside customer, and he went off to prepare some coffee on a small cylinder gas stove. We sat sipping the strong Turkish coffee and looking towards the sea which had become in some curious way a goal to be reached. Across the inlet was the bustling Greek community with its traffic and sense of movement so lacking on this side. The young man's family had a house in that area.

'I don't suppose we shall ever get it back,' he said.

'Surely, when all this is over?'

'Never!' he said with cheerful resignation, 'we do not trust any more. Partition is the only solution.'

'But . . . '

'Don't talk politics,' said Ali, 'let us enjoy our quest.'

Later when I rose to go, there was no question of my being allowed to pay for the coffee. And as I climbed into the old car, the young 'proprietor' waved.

'Come again some time,' he called, 'maybe by then the next storey will be built!' and he laughed cheerfully.

Lion at the Sea Gate, Famagusta

United Nations troops crossing the Green Line in Nicosia

5

The Monastery of Ayios Neophytos

I persuaded Nancy to come along with me to the Enkleistra and Monastery of Ayios Neophytos which is about six miles north-east of Paphos. She has seen many monasteries over the years and her comments on them and their inhabitants were rather guarded. But she came with a good grace, humouring me and feeling perhaps that a day's relaxation from the sterner things of life would not come amiss.

The monastery and its fifteenth-century church has a beautiful setting at the end of a small valley and it is sheltered by low cliffs and sloping hills. Caves are cut in the cliffs and below on flat ground is a permanent spring that is now covered with a stone building. This fine supply of water was the reason no doubt for the choice of the site in the first place. We stopped and looked down at the peaceful scene and it was so still we could hear the bees droning.

Neophytes is a favourite character with the Cypriots. He was born in 1134 in the hills near Kate Lefkara – the town that makes beautiful hand-made lace – and ran away from home when his parents wanted to find him a bride. He became a novice in the Monastery of Chrysostomos which stands below the castle of Buffavento in the Kyrenia Range. Whilst he was here, looking after the vines of the monastery, he learnt to read and write and after five years was promoted to sacristan. Later he left with the intention of finding a solitary retreat and made one attempt to leave the island for Asia Minor, but he failed and finally came to this valley where he found a cave in the cliff-side – and the spring. For a year he worked on the cave, enlarging it into a double chamber; in one he carved a stone table and bench where he slept, and then he tunnelled deeper making space for his grave. In the other chamber he had an altar and dedicated his retreat to the Holy Cross. He lived here for eleven years in almost complete seclusion but finally his friend Basil Kinnamos, the Bishop of Paphos, persuaded him to be ordained and to take a disciple. This was the beginning of the monastery and from that time his reputation as a recluse and holy man brought other ascetics and worshippers. Buildings were erected to accommodate the new community which increased as more pilgrims found their way to the place. But Neophytes was, at heart, a recluse and his love of solitude forced him to vacate the cell he had occupied for forty years and despite his age he set about constructing another one higher up the cliff. He worked at the new cell for many months, and was often in danger from falling rocks. When the place was finished he was completely isolated for the only access was by a ladder which he could draw up.

It was during his earlier life in the caves that he wrote the famous *Ritual Ordinance* which set out the rules for the monastic community he founded, as well as other religious works. He had some very decided views about many things as well as being an ardent patriot. He left a letter relating to the misfortunes of his island at the time, and he says some caustic things, not only about Richard Coeur de Lion whom he calls: 'The King, the Wretch' but the island's own usurper king, Isaac.

Neophytes died when he was eighty and was buried in the niche grave he dug for himself, but five hundred years later the tomb was opened and his bones now lie in the adjoining church. It is still believed by the sick that if they climb into the empty tomb and turn round three times, they will be cured of their illness.

The priest who came hurrying across the monastery courtyard seemed pleased to see us. His long black tunic or *Rasos* was dusty and a little spotted and his crisp brown hair spilled out over his shoulders. He appraised us both – more as women than converts I felt – and led us along the cool corridor and up the stairs. Lemon trees grew in the court, and beyond was the fifteenth-century domed church. The warm-toned sandstone, the deep green of the trees and the brilliant sunlight made a fine picture. It was quiet and still. In the sitting-room we signed the book and had small cups of coffee. A table ran along the centre of the room and there were a couple of bright Victorian sofas. The view from the window down the valley was magnificent.

Later we climbed the steps to Neophytes's caves which are now quite impersonal and have been faced with an arched corridor. The rock sides and ceilings of the caves are covered with paintings of different periods. Neophytes stated that after twenty-four years the Enkleistra was entirely covered with paintings. Since that time several have been re-touched or overpainted and others suffered from mutilation when the Turks conquered the island. In accordance with their religion they scratched out the eyes of many of the saints. The chapel has many beautiful pictures and scenes from the New Testament but the painting of St Neophytes supported by two angels, in the Byzantine style, is arresting and lifelike and it dominates the whole cave. The small area where he lived and worked for so long, with its stone-cut desk and seat, has been left as it was. Collectively, the paintings cover many periods and they give a good opportunity for seeing the changes of style in Byzantine art.

The church is quite large. It is dedicated to the Blessed Virgin Mary and has a double-vaulted roof supported by columns. There are the remains of mural paintings of the fifteenth and sixteenth centuries, with some pleasant small ones around the vault of the aisles. The bones of the Saint and his skull, which is set in a silver case, are in the church, but when a man goes to the trouble of digging or carving his own grave, it seems a little presumptuous to move him – even after five hundred years.

The monk insisted that it was lucky to drink the water from the spring and led me down the stone steps into the tiny vault where the water ran cold and clear out of the hillside. He splashed me with it and the procedure was in danger of becoming anything but a Christian ritual, so I returned to the sunshine and the waiting Nancy. 'Well, if you will go into vaults with Cypriot monks what can you expect!' her glance clearly implied.

I walked along the dimly-lighted street of pleasant bungalows and turned in at the gate of one of the largest of them. Two Greek soldiers stood on guard. I was expected and climbed the steps to a porch crowded with pot-plants. It was the home of a Turkish Cypriot doctor who had defected to the Greek side and he lived here with his wife. A tall man in a grey suit and wearing dark glasses opened the door and led me into an L-shaped room with television, hi-fi, good furniture and many vases of flowers. But there was a stillness, even a bleakness of a house that is not a home. His wife, a pleasant dark woman, served coffee from a silver pot. The doctor still practised and his consulting room was at the side of the house. Most of his clients were Greek Cypriots now, although he assured me some of his own people – the peasants from the outlying countryside – came at night to see him.

He believed that the Turkish Cypriots should have agreed to the terms in the Plaza report that was put forth in March 1965 and could have replaced the Zurich and London Agreements that had broken down. The main points in the Plaza report were that Cyprus should remain independent but renounce its right to choose union with Greece, the island to be demilitarized; and there should be no partition or physical separation of the two communities. Nevertheless the Turkish Cypriots' rights were to be guaranteed by the United Nations, who would install a commissioner in the island for this purpose. The Greeks agreed to the proposal in general, but the Turks turned it down flat. This led to the Makarios Government securing the adoption, by the United Nations Assembly, of a resolution supporting a claim for the independence of Cyprus without any ties with Turkey and to waive its claim to intervene, as set down in the Zurich and London Agreements. So, although no solution for the two sides was found, Makarios gained for himself a small advantage.

The Turks of Ankara, the doctor insisted, were leading the Turkish Cypriots astray. They were instilling in them the need for partition to which the Greek Cypriots would never agree and there would be stalemate *ad infinitum*. 'Perhaps,' he said, 'some day my people will see the sense in trying to co-operate with the Greeks.'

I rose to go, and the doctor came with me to the door.

'Life is easy for you here?' I inquired.

'Yes, why not? Life is quite normal.'

It was very dark outside now and *three* soldiers were guarding the house. By the time I reached the gate the doctor had already disappeared inside and shut the door. There was a certain eeriness about the still, well-kept garden, and the silent guards. The nights, I felt, must be very long in that flower-bedecked bungalow. It takes a certain kind of courage to act in this manner. I walked down the dark street and far ahead was the Green Line, the no-man's-land, and beyond, the Turkish enclave where so many families were crowded together, noisy, uncomfortable, exasperating, heartbreaking – but *alive*.

We went swimming on Christmas Day, but it wasn't the most pleasant dip I have had; and the British U.N. officers asked us to dine that evening. They gave us a fine Christmas dinner complete with champagne and were charming hosts to two females bent on information. Considering that the British soldier is drafted to the job with U.N. on exactly the same pay as he receives anywhere else with the British Army, whilst most other countries pay their men twice as much or more, I felt a little guilty at their lavish hospitality.

The island is large enough not to make one claustrophobic and yet most places are within a day's jaunt in any direction. It was still rather uncertain driving around here however and we received the same contradictory information one is given when contemplating a desert journey; some say it will be a 'piece of cake' whilst others are certain one will be murdered at the start. Certainly a couple of women tourists, driving off the beaten track, had backed their car on to some sort of explosive and landed up in hospital. However we had a beautiful day driving over the winding roads to the north coast where at Polis we turned left and ran for six miles along the coast in search of the Fontana Amoroso, Aphrodite's Fountain of Love. As the road climbed we came to a tiny café set amongst the trees. We left the car for it is necessary to continue on foot.

I often wonder if legends create an atmosphere around a place, or if the atmosphere creates the legend; whichever it might be, the still quiet gully of trees and shrubs makes it impossible not to think of Aphrodite. We climbed to the other side of the little depression where the rocks crowded round a huddle of protecting trees and in the centre was the pool. What is extraordinary is that the famous pool with the maidenhair fern, the trickling water coming from the rock beyond and the huge fig tree which grows out of the bank above, is exactly as it has been described for centuries. It is believed that if you drink the water you will fall in love and that this is the land of beautiful women to whom Aphrodite gave everlasting love to the end of their days. However the place was completely deserted, although a well-worn path led from the pool to the open cliff towards the sea. It fell away sheer leaving flat ground above which makes a fine spot for a picnic.

In ordinary times it would have been possible to continue west along the north coast to Kyrenia but the Kokkina Turkish enclave lies in its path and it was closed at present because of the recent troubles.

We turned off the main Paphos-to-Limassol road on to a track that led towards the hills. It was early and the air was clear and still. Immediately on leaving the main road there was an air of isolation, it seemed that everyone stayed on the main roads as far as possible. The Land-Rover bumped over the rough ground and in the back was Captain Tim Taylor, Major Evelegh's second-in-command. From time to time there was trouble in the Turkish village we were heading for and many incidents, disappearances and murders occurred along this route. The previous summer a Greek taxi-driver with a woman and child passenger, disappeared without trace, and a Turkish policeman, the father of twelve children, was shot dead whilst watching stock. Despite all this, a Greek bus still went through the village twice a day, although no Greek National Guard or member of the Cyprus police were allowed to ride in it.

The surrounding countryside was uncultivated, and bare and deserted as we climbed along the side of the valley. The Yeros river lay far below but the track, now running towards the brow of the hill, made us a sitting target. When we finally came to the high village we stopped beside the concrete terrace of the local café. The Captain was greeted by several old men and we moved into the café which was a rough shed with a couple of large tables and dozens of chairs set around the walls. An old iron stove stood in the centre. One by one, other old men arrived and sat around the wall, watching us intently. They had fine weather-beaten faces, lined and hard as hawks. A young school-teacher acted as interpreter, and various people had grievances that they put to the Captain. No compensation had been settled about the Muktar and his small son from the near-by village who had been murdered; the Greeks bought fruit from the Turks at 50 mils an oke, but gave their own people 73 mils; plans for Government development were going ahead, but because of the troubles the Turks were being left out. So it went on. The UNFICYP men not only clear up many small troubles and act as a go-between with the other side, but they are a safety-valve for pent-up feelings and emotions. Some of the old men were refugees from the village of Khudu near Pitaghu which had been attacked by night. The old men, anonymous behind their dark leathery faces, sat silent most of the time and allowed the younger ones to talk. The Captain listened patiently, and gradually the atmosphere relaxed, a joke or two was made, and cigarettes were passed round.

The Captain could solve some of the domestic problems, or he promised to bring them up with their counterparts on the Greek side. He reminded them of the work on the bridge farther up the road where both Greek and Turkish Cypriots were working side by side. Whenever there was some constructive work of this kind the men worked well together and there should be more of these projects, but as the years go by children are growing up who have never been in contact with the other side.

The Muktar of the village, a wiry old man with a sprightly eye, invited us for breakfast, and we followed him down a cobbled back street to a mud brick bungalow. We sat round a large table in a room taken up entirely by the table, chairs, and a huge upholstered couch. His womenfolk stayed in the kitchen beyond and would not join us. We had coffee, orange juice, grilled kidneys and liver, cheese, chips and beer. The old man, indignant and gay in turns, noticed a locket round my neck which contains a tiny copy of the Koran. With a flourish he opened it and began to 'read' – although the print is hardly discernible even with a strong magnifying glass! Finally, with a pious flourish, he closed the little volume and handed it back to me.

When we left the bungalow the whole village moved in to see us off, and the old Muktar waved an expansive 'good-bye' from the steps.

'A nice old boy,' said the Captain as we drove off.

I nodded, but the Greeks, I felt, had met their match in him.

6

Cities of the South

On our return journey we stopped for a few days' luxury and warmth at the new hotel which lies just east of Limassol. The Miramare is under the same management as the Ledra Palace and has everything from air conditioning to central heating; each room has its own bathroom and their balconies look over the terrace and the sea. All the hotel lacked at this time was clients and the large bars and public rooms were empty. The following May, however, the tourists had returned and it presented a very different sight.

Limassol is growing fast, for as well as the port there are large factory and commercial areas and the new residential town. Along the coast road several canning factories for fruit and soft drinks have been opened and although there are no docks and quays here the port handles all the shipping of the carobs, fruit and vegetables from the surrounding countryside. In view of all this it is perhaps the most cosmopolitan of the cities and its infusion of new blood is producing many of the island's best brains.

Despite the air of sophistication and prosperity, on one spring day each year the town goes quite mad when Limassol's carnival brings people from all over the island to take part in, or watch, the procession of crazy floats and all kinds of mobile fantasia. Suddenly the town is transformed into a blaze of colour and there is an air of abandoned festivity that turns it into a cross between Coney Island and Las Vegas. I never felt quite the same again about this pompous city, or treated it with the respect it expects after such a day!

Nancy had already seen the famous Keo factory whose beer, wine and brandies are the best known in the island. It is also the oldest company and was started back in 1927 with a capital of £25,000 – now it runs into millions. Today forty per cent of the wines exported from the island are Keo and in the season half a million okes of grapes are crushed each day. A pipe-line runs out from the shore to the sea where the wine is loaded on to ships at the rate of ninety tons an hour.

We, together with the Germans, are the best customers, although France was way ahead before the advent of the Common Market. The large winery is just west of the town and it adjoins the Turkish Cypriot sector. Most of the political troubles pass right over the Company's head and although a much larger percentage of the employees are Greek Cypriots there is no trouble between the workers, which is the case with other large-scale organizations such as the mines and the Palestine Fruit Plantations. It would seem there is a lesson to be learned here, and if the island could consolidate its workers, Greek and Turkish, with more large-scale projects, the merging of the two communities, which is so important, would become effective.

There is a friendly naturalness about Cypriots that makes even a visit to the factories a pleasant jaunt and it was like some Bacchante dream to wander through the great vaults, feeling completely dwarfed by the rows of huge barrels where the wines were quietly fermenting. When I was leaving they gave me a bottle of the famous Commanderia – vintage indeed as it was one hundred years old. It is claimed to be the oldest wine in the world and the same process is used today as then.

The name Commanderia comes from the Commandery of the Knights of St John of Jerusalem who owned Kolossi Castle and its estates just west of here. The land north of the Castle where the vines grow is one of the richest areas in the island. The Hospitallers were given the state of Kolossi by King Hugh I in 1210 not long after the Latin occupation of the island. After the fall of Acre in 1291 Cyprus became the headquarters of the Order and Henry II placed them, together with the Templars, in occupation of Limassol. The Knights became immensely wealthy, not only from the sale of their wines, but from their sugar plantations. They continued to expand, developing large estates and setting up villages. The present castle was built in 1454 and it figured prominently in the struggles between Charlotte and her half-brother James for the throne. At the beginning of the sixteenth century the castle was given to Cardinal Mario Cornaro, the brother of Queen Catherine; and this family held it until the invasion of the Turks. Now it belongs to the State and stands surrounded by the British Sovereign Base Area of Akrotiri.

Nancy had never seen the castle except at a distance and we drove out one bright clear morning. It is a beautiful and impressive place with a great keep rising eighty feet. There are crenellated battlements and a high drawbridge. Tall cypresses contrast vividly with the sandstone which the strong sunlight turns to gold. It is solid and square and entirely different from all the other castles in the island. Despite its impressiveness, it is not so very large. There are three storeys and the ramparts. The lower section has three vaulted rooms that were used by the Knights as storage, with a well below in case of siege. The entrance to the castle is by the drawbridge on the first floor that leads into the great Main Hall which, at the moment, is completely empty. On the right as you enter is a large mural of the Crucifixion and the coat of arms of Louis de Magnac, Grand Commander of Cyprus who built the castle. The second room was the kitchen and except for a large stone fireplace it is also empty. In one corner of the building is a spiral staircase, cunningly made out of the stone that leads to the floor above where there are two beautifully vaulted rooms each measuring about forty-five by twenty feet. Small slit windows are sunk into the walls, which are about ten feet thick, and on one side also sunk into the wall is a privy. Both rooms have magnificent fireplaces, they are French in design and character and both have the coat of arms of Louis de Magnac. The small staircase continues to the battlements above where we had a marvellous view of the countryside and the salt lake of Limassol.

The castle was restored in 1933 which accounts for its good condition. Wooden floors could be built between each storey and may have been there at one time. If this was done the castle would make a beautiful museum or gallery.

We wandered out below the cypresses again and into the remains of a large vaulted barn which had been a sugar mill in the Knights' days. An old medieval aqueduct near by is still used for irrigation. I looked at the golden castle, the cypresses and the intervening ground, falling away on different levels.

'What a marvellous garden you could make here!' I said.

My companion gave me a quizzical look, 'Possessions are not for travellers,' she said.

* * * *

Larnaca is my favourite town on the south coast; it is *gemütlish* and unexpected like the contrary cat. It is also more of a bay than a port, even though from early times travellers arrived here by ship. There are plans afoot to build a harbour for yachts which will make it a serious rival to Kyrenia, for not only is it on the warmer side of the island, but it has a Riviera quality all its own. The wide promenade runs along the sea-shore where café chairs and tables are overhung by palms.

Zeno who founded the Stoic school of philosophy was born here in 336 B.C. and it is incongruous that the man whose austere philosophy influenced both the Greek and Roman world, should have come from this luxury-loving island. The town was founded by the Phoenicians, although according to legend Noah's great-grandson Kittim settled here after the deluge. It suffered, along with the other ports, from the raiding Arabs but during the Middle Ages when the Genoese took Famagusta, the town was rebuilt and used as a port of embarkation for the Holy Land Pilgrimages. Then it was known as Salines because of the salt lake near by. Later, when it was used as the main port for Nicosia, consuls and merchants settled in the town and it became very prosperous. They lived in great luxury and entertained lavishly. There was one British Consul in particular who built the finest house in Cyprus with a saloon in which he could entertain five hundred guests. His way of life led him into debt and he owed money to many of the town's leading citizens. One day he arranged a large banquet and invited all his creditors. Everyone accepted, for they hoped not only to have a good meal but that he would settle his debts. When everyone arrived he excused himself for a moment and slipping out of the house went to the shore where a ship was waiting. He had previously arranged with the captain to bring aboard his most valuable possessions and as soon as he arrived the ship set sail. In the meantime, the guests were waiting impatiently for their host, but not only was he never seen again but there was no dinner either!

The Four Lanterns Hotel has been given a face-lift and it is still the best hotel in the town. Once again we were presented with the usual hotel form to fill in.

'Why?' I asked plaintively, 'do they want to know *everything* about one's family tree?' and when I came to a demand for my age, I put '100', in defiance.

I handed the paper over to a pretty little teenage receptionist. She watched me, fascinated, as I mounted the stairs with our two suitcases.

'Well,' she called after me, at last, 'I hope *I* look as good as you when I'm *your* age!'

The most important monument is the Church of St Lazarus which was built to enshrine his tomb. It is a large white structure with a high belfry and was reconstructed in its original form in the seventeenth century. It is believed that Lazarus, after his resurrection at Bethany, was put with his two sisters into a light craft and sent out to sea. They finally drifted in and landed near Larnaca and Lazarus was consecrated Bishop by the Apostles who happened to be on the spot. He continued to live in the town and was buried here, but in the ninth century, his remains were discovered and taken to Constantinople, to be stolen later by the French and removed to Marseilles – where they are to this day. Although the sarcophagus is empty it is still considered a holy place and venerated by the local people. The most unusual icon is the *Raising of Lazarus* which depicts a man holding his nose whilst opening the coffin which recalls the words, 'Lord, by this time he stinketh, for he hath been dead four days'.

It was becoming a not-very-pleasant game, spotting the Turkish sector and even though Larnaca had changed less than the other cities, tensions ran very high around the Artemis Avenue area and it was causing the U.N. troops some anxiety. It was impossible for us to drive along the avenue alone and we collected two Swedish officers. The long straight avenue was bristling with armoured cars that patrol day and night. On one side the Greeks had turned the bungalows into bunkers and bomb traps and on the other, where the ground rose slightly, the Turks had reinforced it with sandbags and recently erected bunkers. It was an uncomfortable feeling driving between the two lines so close together for we were a very conspicuous target.

West of Artemis Avenue is the salt lake and the Tekke of Umm Haram. For centuries the lake was a great source of income to the island for the salt was gathered into piles and later exported to other countries.

Large flocks of flamingoes settle on the shores of the lake and on the far shore stands the Tekke of Umm Haram whose minarets, domes and palms reflect in the water. The Tekke, the flamingoes and the blue-grey of the lake gave the landscape a distinct eastern touch.

Despite the belief that women are second-class citizens in the Muslim world, every one of the passing ships dips its flag as it sights the Tekke. Umm Haram, it is believed, was a female relative of Mahomet. She was married to Umbada or the Pot Bellied who was Cadi of Palestine and came to the island in A.D. 694 with one of the many expeditions that raided the island. It was customary in those days for women to accompany the raiders, acting as nurses and helpmates to the men – a kind of Muslim *vivandière* perhaps.

The party arrived near Larnaca and set off on mules for the interior. They had reached the lake when the Genoese attacked them and Umm Haram fell from her mule and broke her neck . . . 'falling from her beast she broke her pellucid neck and yielded up her victorious soul, and in that fragrant spot was at once buried'. Natural enough as it is the custom to bury Muslims before the sun sets.

Such is the story told by every traveller who visited the spot and the tomb looks much as they describe it, although now it is covered with a dome, and incorporated in the mosque. The tomb consists of an enormous stone laid across two upright ones which were, until recently, believed to be of prehistoric origin. Their convenient presence was explained by the story that Umm Haram, whilst in Syria, admired three stones belonging to a monk who, knowing quite well they could not be transported, gave them to her. Umm Haram accepted the gift saying she would send for them some time. On the evening of her death the stones appeared and were set up, one at her feet, another at her head and the third suspended above her.

We drew up in an outer court and walked through the gardens shaded by palms and orange trees. The Tekke is now in Greek hands but the whole place still has a feeling of peace and tranquillity. A young Greek Cypriot caretaker showed us over the mosque and the shrine.

'You don't have to take off your shoes,' he said to me with surprise as we came to the entrance.

'I shall, just the same,' I said, in deference to the old lady.

The shrine was placed over the tomb in 1760 and in the nineteenth century the Turkish Governor of the island built the mosque which covers it. We crossed the open arena of the mosque and passed through the arched doorway. In the small enclosure the tomb is covered with a heavily embroidered cloth. The upright stones are swathed in black velvet, giving the impression that the top one is suspended in the air. The device is often used both by the Turks and the Greeks and it seems unnecessary, for the whole structure is impressive enough without this mumbo jumbo.

In 1930 the second wife of King Hussein of the Hedjaz, who was a Turk, died in Cyprus and was buried in the Tekke. Is it perhaps that the Tomb has lost some of its sanctity? When we left I offered the young man some money 'for the mosque'. He looked puzzled.

'I can't take it,' he said at last.

'Why not? It's for the mosque – for the church.'

'But' he said, seeking a word, 'it's not *our* church.'

I gave it up. 'There's one God – somewhere,' I said – and pocketing the money climbed back into the Land-Rover.

A few miles farther west along the coast is the village of Kiti which is probably the Kittam that was founded by Noah's great-grandson. Later Charles de Lusignan owned the town but he paid for his loyalty to Queen Charlotte when her half-brother James II took it away from him. Now, it is a quiet little place with one beautiful jewel – the Church of Panagia Angelokotes (Built by the Angels). The domed building is constructed on the ruins of an early Byzantine basilica and is set off by a huge tree. In the conch of the apse is the real treasure, the mosaic of the Virgin Mary and Child with the archangels Michael and Gabriel.

We were fortunate for we could not find the caretaker with the key of the church and so it was already late in the afternoon when a small boy let us in. The rays of the sun at the moment were slanting obliquely through the windows and bringing to life, in a startling fashion, the life-size group. The mosaic is considered the best in the island and dates from the seventh century, but few people could have the luck to see it as we did at this moment. The Virgin holds the Child in her left hand and the effect is one of naturalness not often found in mosaics, and even the archangels are graceful and relaxed. The wings are beautifully worked, giving an impression of peacock's feathers with the 'eye', and the whole composition is set off magnificently by a background of fine cubes which was startling now in the slanting sunlight that turned it into a cloth of gold.

There are other things to see in the old church, and the attached chapel which belonged to the medieval family of Gibelet has a fine carved gravestone of a lady; and their coat of arms is built into the wall. But at this time everything else was overshadowed by the mosaic. Even the small boy was overawed by the sight.

'Come,' he said at last, 'to look again at the Virgin. For when the sun goes, everyone sleeps.'

They are there, all over the island. Little communities of the Turks each with the same problems and with individual dramas. I stood watching her coming towards me along the muddy street. She was a tiny woman, nicely rounded and with a smooth unlined face that was the colour of honey. Short brown hair fell in easy waves and made a chestnut frame to her face. She wore a checked cotton shirt and brown trousers and carried a brief-case as she came down the narrow street in the Turkish village – the silence of Turkish villages, no matter how many people are around was becoming very familiar – she wasn't smiling but this was no lack of friendship, and every gesture was sincere. I had been waiting outside a small building and when she opened the arched double doors a small general store lay beyond. There was a counter to one side with a safe beyond and the rest of the

Bellapais

Janus near the Roman fishpool near Zambousa

Glafkos Clerides, Archbishop Makarios and Polycarpos Georgadis watching a parade, Nicosia

space was taken up with all kinds of goods. The village was in the centre of a Turkish farming enclave, in a very unsettled area. Madame was the widow of a prominent Turkish Cypriot and when he died she took over most of his responsibilities and was now running the large farm as well.

We sat, one each side of the counter, and she called to a small boy who was watching from the door to bring two cups of tea. She reiterated the usual complaints, the unfairness, the lack of supplies, selling of goods for less than the Greeks were given, the petty irritations, the indignities of the women being searched as they went through the Famagusta Gate in Nicosia; and the many incidents that could blow up into something big at any time. A perpetual watching.

As we talked she became slightly relaxed, although she had disciplined herself to keep all the important problems foremost in her mind and was not interested in mere pleasantries. Perhaps she had to make an extra effort being a woman, and there certainly was the woman's no-compromise approach.

'I go on with the farm work,' she said, 'and look after my people. Fighting – fighting to regain our rights to be allowed to live as free human beings. You would not think it was much to ask.'

'And what if there have to be compromises?'

'Compromises! We ask for our rights as they were – nothing more, nothing less.'

'If, and when, this happens,' I asked, 'will you then be able to live – as before?'

She looked at me intently. 'You have seen a lot. Do you think that after everything, we could ever trust again?'

'But that is awful! It means the only solution would be partition and if the island is divided into entirely separate areas, surely the weaker side will become weaker still?'

She gave a short laugh and spread her hands in a shrugging gesture. 'What other course?' she asked softly.

When I made a move to go she stood up also. 'I shall come with you in the Land-Rover,' she said, 'and show you round the village. You can drop me near the field where I was working.'

We climbed into the vehicle and talked of ordinary things. Suddenly she looked pretty and animated – too young not to be having any fun. The village was flat and dull with a series of mud houses. She pointed to the ruins of an old church.

'It goes back a long time,' she said, 'but the village has been in Turkish hands for centuries.'

We stopped finally near the field where the men were working, and she climbed out.

'That's hard work for a little person like you,' I said.

'I'm fortunate in having something to work at,' she said flatly.

'Good luck.' I sounded puerile and inadequate.

She looked at me gravely. 'If you return come and see us in "Little Cyprus",' she said, smiling slightly and then turned towards the others.

I hope it will be possible.

7

Siege in the Sun

Famagusta is the last large town on the south coast, a hotch-potch of Greek commercialism, tourism and a hectic building programme – a very far cry from the sleepy seaside village of Varosha of early years. The beautiful long curve of sandy beach is being completely hemmed in by large high hotels and apartment houses, that block out the sun far too early in the day. But the medieval city to the east, preserved within its fine walls is miraculously escaping the building fury for the time being. It was with a sense of relief that we crossed the causeway into the old city, although even today it is overshadowed in some odd way by the tragic siege of 1571; and by the ghost of its defender Marc Antonio Bragadino. The epic of the siege and of Bragadino's personal bravery puts it amongst the most glorious in history.

Centuries before, as far back as the third century B.C. there was a community here; and the Greeks from Salamis are known to have re-peopled it in the seventh century, though why this was necessary is not known. By the time of the early crusades it was little more than a walled castle with a village and a small harbour, but with the fall of Acre in 1291 King Henry II allowed the Christian refugees to settle here. From that time the city began to prosper and became one of the richest in the Levant as the nobility and the merchants vied with each other to display their wealth and lavish hospitality. It takes little imagination to visualize the splendour and colour of the charming little walled city. This golden age came abruptly to an end following an incident that was initially quite trivial.

It was the custom of the Lusignan kings to receive the crown of Cyprus in the Cathedral of Nicosia, and the crown of Jerusalem – which was of less importance – in St Nicholas of Famagusta. During the ceremony the king rode to the cathedral on a horse which was led by representatives of both Genoa and Venice; the latter holding the left rein, and the former the right-hand one. During the coronation of Peter II in 1372, the king appeared as usual on horseback but the Venetian representative laid hold on the right-hand rein; whereupon the Genoese representative sprang forward to stake his claim. Immediately there was a scuffle which led to a riot and during the fight many Genoese were killed. The coronation broke up in disorder.

When news of the affair finally reached Genoa, a fleet was dispatched immediately to avenge the insult and also the deaths. In due course it arrived off Famagusta and attacked the city which finally fell. The Genoese changed the whole face of the city for it became heavily armed and little more than a fortress whose wealth and commerce gradually dwindled. Such was the position of Famagusta when King James returned to the island in 1464; he attacked the city and drove the Genoese out.

Later under the Venetians the city regained some of its former importance but in 1570 Sultan Selim II who was known as 'The Sot' because of his love of wine, decided to capture the island. It has been said that the famous Cypriot wines were his main objective! He sent a fleet, under the command of General Leon Mustafa and the invasion duly took place. Nicosia was the first large town to fall and then Famagusta surrendered, after a siege of four months. The siege was concentrated and vicious and during that time there were attacks and counter-attacks, slow starvation and, it is said, 100,000 cannon balls landed in the walled city. By the time Bragadino finally surrendered, it had cost General Mustafa the lives of eighty thousand men. The stipulation of their surrender was that Bragadino's men and the entire population of the city should be allowed to embark and sail for Crete. To this Mustafa agreed, but once he entered the city and saw the small and weak company that had kept his army at bay for so long and had been responsible for so many deaths, he became insane with fury. He ordered Bragadino to be seized, his nose and ears cut off, and after many tortures, he was flayed alive.

During all this frightful experience, Bragadino remained calm until the moment he died. The rest of the company was hewn to pieces together with the Christians who were embarking on the ship. Later they stuffed Bragadino's body with straw and hung it up for everyone to see; and it was finally paraded along the coast of Syria as a sign of the final fall of Famagusta. After the parade the skin was put in a box and sent to Constantinople where it was placed in the arsenal. Many years later Bragadino's children were able to buy the pitiful remains of their father for a large sum, and they were taken to Venice where they now rest in the Church of S.S. Giovanni e Paolo. If the Venetian rule over the island had been unpraiseworthy, the defence of Famagusta in the hands of Marc Antonio Bragadino and his brave men did much to vindicate their name.

With the fall of Famagusta there was little further opposition to the Turks who were able to take over the whole island. But the cruelty and treacherousness of the affair is one of the foullest scars on the rule of the Turks in Cyprus. During the years that followed the conquerors repaired the walls but little else, and the city was used mainly as a prison. When the British arrived in 1878 they found many prisoners within the walls, most of them having been deported from Turkey. Amongst them was Subh-i-Ezel the successor to Mirza Ali Mohammad who founded the Babi sect. The British released him but he decided to stay on in the city and lived here until he died at the age of eighty-two. Gunnis tells of his two establishments and two wives and how, promptly at four each afternoon the first wife escorted him to the house of the second and handed him over. Then twenty-four hours later, at the same time, the second wife brought him back again.

It is impossible not to be reminded of General Bragadino in the old city. The presence of ruins and the expanse of razed ground accentuate the desolate air, although much of this damage was done during the last century when whole buildings and churches were torn down and the stones transported to build Port Said and its quays. The ramparts remained, however, and they are amongst the finest examples of medieval architecture, comparable with Ragusa and Carcassone. East of the Sea Gate with its large stone lion that is credited with miraculous powers, is the Citadel. It was originally built in the fourteenth century with four round towers and a moat. Famagusta has often been described by early travellers as being in the sea and this would have been the impression when the moats were flooded. Over the main entrance of the Citadel is a carving of the winged lion of the Republic with the name of the Venetian Captain Nicolo Foscarini who rebuilt part of the second floor. This is Othello's Tower. Although Shakespeare merely mentions, 'A seaport in Cyprus', Othello could have been the Lieutenant Governor of Cyprus, Christoforo Moro, for his name and coat of arms of three mulberries sable, can mean both mulberry tree or Moor. Beyond the entrance is a sheltered court with old stones and a few trees. It leads to the Great Hall or refectory which is a large high gallery ninety-five feet long. A rather makeshift café was being set up in anticipation of summer tourists. Stone stairs lead to the tower ramparts which overlook the harbour, and the atmosphere engendered by the intimate court, the fine old hall and the solid ramparts, is quickly dispelled by the small blue observation post and the inevitable U.N. flag!

The square of the cathedral is the pivot of the town as it must always have been. The cathedral is now a mosque and known as S. Sophia. It is, together with the S. Sophia in Nicosia, one of the finest examples of early fourteenth-century Gothic art and both have escaped the 'improvements' of later generations which makes them unique. When they became mosques the interiors were stripped of all rich decorations and the frescoes were painted over. Magnificent as they must have been formerly, the austerity of the interiors give a special beauty to the buildings today.

The façade of S. Sophia towers above the square and looks down on the untidy square of cafés, market and small shops. The triple porch has straight side gabled canopies and above the centre is a magnificent window with a circle tracery. From one of the corner towers a minaret rises. The effect is lighter, airier than the sister cathedral in Nicosia and the sun strikes through the tracery on to the tombs and the Moslem *minber*. A few medieval tombstones still remain in the north aisle but the Turks removed most of them in 1571 and threw them into the sea.

Across the square is the site of the Lusignan Palace where their kings lived, but there is little but the outline of the area and a skeleton façade with three arches that are supported by columns. It was in front of the palace that General Bragadino was tortured.

We sat in the square drinking Bel Kola and were slightly under a cloud, for going in search of the ruined Church of St Francis we had stumbled on a building which must have been used for more dubious purposes, and we were firmly escorted back to the main square. The cathedral dominates from all angles, the doors were closed and sun caught the whole sandstone face lighting up the tracery. So many people had passed beneath the portals, James II and his small son to their last rest, and Catherine his queen when she gave her final act of abdication.

A few men sat in the café and they were all Turks for no Greek would venture into the city. There were no vehicles and the town was empty and still, for there is little commerce or incentive for anyone to stay in the town who doesn't work in the harbour.

Later when we drove back to the Land Gate the Turkish policeman stopped us with a cheerful grin. He glanced inside the Land-Rover. 'Come again,' he said, 'it's quite like old times!' and he waved us on.

*   *   *   *

Famagusta, January 1968

Dear Belkiss,

We have been having a 'most unusual' cold spell and there is snow on the plain and in Nicosia.

Under the amnesty agreement the extra Greek soldiers left yesterday (15th) by ship. I think even the Greek Cypriots are thankful to see them go. It is the same old thing, 'We might not do it so well, but we'd rather do it ourselves.'

I finally called on Pol Georghiou as you suggested. His work is fascinating and I now remember seeing an exhibition of his at the Lefevre in London. I suppose he's the only Cypriot artist with an international name?

He is very broken about the death of his wife and is living for the time being with his sister in an apartment opposite our hotel. She took me to see his old home which is one of the typical Cypriot style houses, there are not many left now. I fell in love with it, high doors leading into a wide hall that runs out to an enclosed court at the back, a beautiful arrangement. Lemon and orange trees grow here and wooden stairs run to the floor above. Large gracious rooms with his paintings and so many things they obviously collected together. No wonder he cannot brace himself to go back. Artists and creative people who are lucky enough to find someone to team or mate with, do become terribly dependent for certain things. He liked me and his sister said I 'did him good'; it's being little and noncommittal I suppose!

I'm terribly afraid – about the house – that I might find some such place and fall in love with it, and there we go again. . . .

The hotel is the only warm place, the people here are just not geared for the few months of cold weather.

I went over to Dhekelia, the second British Sovereign Base area where they have excellent recording studios for the British Forces Broadcasting unit and did an interview with my old pal Douggie George who used to be in Libya. I've built up a fraternity all over the world and it gets larger and larger.

As soon as the weather is a little warmer I shall look for more economical lodgings, probably in the Kyrenia area.

I am sorry you can't come yet but naturally the family comes first. However Beirut is very near so don't give up hope!

8

The Little Hut

> 'I should like to be those two flying swallows
> Who are carrying clay to nest in the eaves of your house.'

Nancy had settled in an hotel in Kyrenia hoping for peace and quiet to 'get on with her work' whilst I now have an establishment; a Little Hut that was the servants' quarters in the garden of a large house. It could be one of those cantonment bungalows of India of the Raj – a row of rooms opening on to a veranda with a tiny kitchen at the back overhung by an old mulberry tree. We are on the outskirts of the small village of Ayios Georgios that lies three miles west of Kyrenia. Above us towers the castle of St Hilarion perching on a high crag, it changes colour several times during the day and in the clear air appears to come very close. Nancy Verey the occupant of the big house, with her sister who is away, is an Englishwoman with a sense of humour and an affinity with animals which we have in common. There are three cats, a Labrador-type dog, and a seventeen-year-old duck named Donald. They all started life as strays (even the duck was rescued from a bad home), for the British who live here are a natural target for all foundlings. Cypriots have an aversion to killing animals, especially cats and so the island is over-run by them.

Each Wednesday Maroula, a smiling little gnome of a *femme de ménage* with no language but Greek, arrives and completely disorganizes my afternoon. She scatters Dettol around with cheerful abandon and talks incessantly, but whether she is saying 'Down with the British', 'Up with Makarios', or what a sloven I am, it's not easy to tell. And once a month a solemn little man comes and sprays all our water butts. They have completely stamped out malaria on the island and mean to keep it so.

The garden is beautiful, full of colour but not too organized.

At the moment it is dazzling with mimosa and a cascade of blooms from a Banksia rose. The Bougainvillaea will soon completely cover the Little Hut with its magenta flowers. The surrounding fields merge into a soft grey-green as old olive trees disappear into the distance. It is very peaceful except for the occasional braying of a donkey or a cock who crows far into the night. Now I don't have to pack each time we want to make a trip of a few days – just turn the key. There have been many of these temporary homes and I remember them all with pleasure, for there is none of the worry attached to a home of one's own.

Nearer St Hilarion is a small Greek village and the Turks in the castle occasionally lob a few shells beyond the village – just as a reminder! Nancy Verey tells me that she had a large mimosa tree cut down during the 1964 troubles so that she could watch the fighting along the ridge whilst she was making breakfast.

Lapithos lies just a few miles to the west. It is a pretty Italian-type village that climbs the slopes and is famous for its lemons and is a great haunt of homosexuals. It was once the capital and one of its kings was a friend of Alexander the Great. but any remains and traces are down on the shore at Lambousa. As well as the lemon groves they make the huge red earthenware oil jars that are sometimes placed on their sides and turned into ovens. One sees them beside the houses or cafés, although now they are seldom used.

It is a relief to be away from the cosiness of Kyrenia which is admittedly picturesque but slightly claustrophobic. The horseshoe-shaped harbour now has several small yachts as well as the fishing craft and the quay is cluttered with tables and chairs that belong to the wayside cafés. On the other side the castle's bastions give extra shelter and a leaning minaret stands isolated in what is now the Greek quarter. Little can be done to change this focal point of the town for the small buildings lining the harbour are 'protected' and there to stay, which is as well for developers are at work on the rest of the town and along the coast each side. Behind the harbour is the tightly packed old part of the town backed by the narrow main street. On the sea front the larger hotels attract an increasing number of tourists each year. The castle's solid walls rise from the deep moat which is now a sunny sheltered place with peppercorn and eucalyptus trees. In place of the old drawbridge a causeway has been built which leads through the arch up to the main barbican. The British used the castle as a prison and a police training school, but later it was handed over to the Department of Antiquities and it has become a great tourist attraction. Already the tourists were returning and a few more could be seen each morning sunbathing on the Dome's veranda.

In a small building beside the castle's causeway overlooking the harbour is the custodian's office where Janus copes with the visitors. He is of medium height with the chunky strength of many Cypriots, light crisp hair and the pleasant square face one so often sees in the carved busts in the museum. He has worked in the Department since British days and a few Anglo-Saxon mannerisms have rubbed off on him, as they have done on other members of the Government Services. He has the archaeologist's attitude which is impervious to any political upsets and tensions. His duties include keeping a watchful eye on all antiquities in the area and sometimes on his day off we go in the Land-Rover to inspect a castle or the work on the restoration of frescoes. Or, following a rumour we'd trek across fields looking for signs of a private 'dig', for the Department controls all archaeological digging, and works of art must be registered with them. Just as it is necessary to have permission to take any antiquities out of the island.

One day I persuaded Janus to come with me to see the famous Asinou Church which is set on the northern slopes of Troodos. The Church is one of the most interesting Byzantine structures in the island and we stopped at Nikitari for the village priest here keeps the key. It is situated three miles farther on, set in gentle folds of the hills and suddenly one sees it, quite alone on a small platform and overlooking the Asinou river. There are no other buildings in sight. It is small, tiny in fact, with an added protective roof. The original part is twelfth century and later the domed narthex was added which makes the proportions quite perfect. On entering the tiny structure, the effect is breathtaking for the entire interior is covered with brilliant frescoes of every imaginable subject and style. They could never have looked better for recently the experts from the

'Center of Byzantine Studies of Dumbarton Oaks, U.S.A.', have been cleaning the entire interior. The island is a paradise for these people who have been working on several of the churches.

There is a real galaxy here, all the old favourites and many that were new to me, with donors dressed in great splendour, and a strange twelfth-century wall-painting of St Mary the Egyptian reputed to be the oldest painting of the saint surviving in the island. According to legend she was an actress of ill-repute who was converted at the Holy Sepulchre in Jerusalem and then disappeared into the desert where she stayed in complete isolation for forty-five years.

Seldom has a church seemed so isolated as it stands surrounded by the rising hills and one wonders what prompted the choice of such a spot, although according to popular tradition their insistence on the name Panagia tis Asinou is the only existing evidence that this was the position of the ancient city of Asine founded by a group of Greek emigrants in the eleventh century B.C.

On our return we drove down to the sea-shore at Lambousa which is now a military zone; and the Monastery of Akhiropietos (Built without Hands) is a barracks and out of bounds. The Virgin is reputed to have brought the entire building over from Asia Minor in a single night. Janus managed to have a cursory look round, for he wanted to make sure the soldiers were not damaging anything in the church, but the boys had taken over the monastery and left the church alone. There is an old Cypriot legend that the shroud of Christ was in the church but a princess of the House of Savoy took it away to the Turin Cathedral where it is now.

On the shore near by are the fascinating Roman fish ponds. The Romans cut a large square pool out of the rock at the water's edge, with channels cleverly designed to let fresh water in but making it impossible for the fish to escape. Now the pond is half filled with stones, but cleared it would be a wonderful and safe swimming pool.

We finished the day eating freshly grilled mullet at a fisherman's café at Vavilas which is a small inlet to the west. We sipped the harsh white wine, and behind us was Kornos, the last peak at the end of the Kyrenia Range. It is pink and grey and has a *living* quality accentuated by the ever-changing colours; as we watched it became fiery red in the setting sun.

The day has been beautiful – but so heartbreaking that my brain seems blown about by a ninety-mile-an-hour gale. I collected Nancy and we set off to find the Turkish village of Trapesa a few miles inland from the coast and east of Kyrenia. A couple of years earlier when there were battles and massacres the Turks of Trapesa had fled to other Turkish villages and enclaves, leaving the village completely deserted. No one knew where the track to the village had been and when we stopped to inquire, there was some confusion for the name means 'bank' and they tried to send us back to Barclays in Kyrenia!

It was late February now and the ground was already bursting with wild flowers of every kind; they come with the suddenness of desert flowers after rain and all round us were patches of blue, pink and red. The asphodel cast mauve shadows and the tiny wild cyclamen formed small closed groups. Aphrodite's legend becomes very feasible at such a time.

As we turned off the coast road on to a rough track the solitary castle of Buffavento loomed ahead, and already there was a deserted air. We passed three barns, padlocked and empty. We saw no one. The track led from here to Trapesa and now it had completely disintegrated. We could just follow its apparent direction along a sharp little valley until the end. Faint indications showed that the track had veered round and taken a narrow hairpin bend up the other side, but several landslides had cut the track in two. Nothing but a Land-Rover or a jeep could have tackled the climb and we negotiated the deep ravine and uncertain banks in silence. I am always surprised at my passenger's faith at such times and I sent up a prayer of thanks to Nancy's innate good sense in keeping quiet – and holding on!

Finally we edged up on to a flat platform which fell away on three sides and was backed by the mountain range beyond. As we turned, the whole panorama of the coast line, below and on each side, stretched before us; it was a magnificent position.

Over the flat surface were clumps of ruins distorted by blast and fire and very different from the mellowed ruins of antiquity that cover the island elsewhere. Some of the walls were still standing but the doors, windows and roofs had all disappeared, leaving only the charred rafters. We stopped beside a modern tap set in a concrete base with a plaque commemorating its erection by H.M.G. and this was the only thing on the whole plateau that was intact and undamaged. Even at such times folk in hot climates retain their respect for water.

We drove towards the first mound of buildings that had formed a small square. The ruin of the largest house still had its outside stone stairs standing and near by a vine struggled to grow over a broken pillar belonging to the village café. Through a gaping hole in another building a huge grinding stone lay at an ungainly angle.

The ground rose slightly towards the schoolhouse which stood apart. It was an oblong structure taller than the others and with bullet-spattered walls. The lettering over the entrance was broken and unintelligible. The door had gone and the windows were mere holes. Nothing whatever remained inside except the blackboard which had fallen at one end but still had faint tracings of a child's sums. Near by two young peach trees were coming into bloom and the fresh colour and persistent growth were unexpected – and pathetic. But these alone gave continuity to the surrounding chaos.

Nearer the plateau edge a stone-built stable had received less harsh treatment than the other buildings and there were several small goats hemmed in by a fence of broken brushwood. We looked around, could anyone live in a place so full of ghosts? There was no house standing and undoubtedly the owner of the goats came up each day from the plain below.

We wondered where they all were, those people who used to waken each day to this beautiful panorama, and this mellow quiet? In the clear fresh sunlight it was impossible to believe in the violent hates that could make this kind of desolation possible; this stupid waste of effort. Everything of substance has gone leaving only a touch of violence in the air; and the things that remain, apart from the peach tree and the struggling vine, are the many tiny children's sandals made of plastic which not even time can eradicate.

. . . . .

Green Monday dawned warm and sunny and with a stillness that made grey-green olive trees behind the Little Hut hang like a velvet drape. It was the Orthodox Church's first day of Lent and Greek families treat it as a holiday, going off into the fields and especially near the sea-shore, where they eat fresh uncooked vegetables and fruit and drink white wine. Picnic groups sat amongst the wild flowers and it is a herald or confirmation of spring, for it was from Cyprus that the first flush of spring burst upon the earth when Aphrodite lived here with Cupid.

A few days later there was a joint celebration for the Turkish Cypriots when Kurban Bayram, one of the main Moslem holidays, coincided with the lifting of the ban by Makarios of the road blocks and other restrictions. It was a great day as families were reunited, some after a period of four years. The lifting of the ban on students abroad immediately brought three plane loads from Turkey when many of them walked in on their families completely unannounced. Cars that had been laid up owing to petrol restrictions, now took to the road and families who had previously fled from their farms with few possessions returned for the first time. In some cases they found the place in ruins, looted and with every movable thing taken away.

We were bathing in the small cove near the Little Hut when a family of six Turks from Nicosia drove up in an old car. They left the vehicle and walked to the rocky headland where they sat for a long time watching the movement of the waves which they had not seen for four years.

The onlooker is relieved at the lifting of the ban; now perhaps things can begin to return to normal, and his first reaction is that anything is better than the present stalemate. When the Turkish leader, Dr Kuchuk, announces that the Cyprus problem cannot be solved by the removal of a few barricades and restrictions without the return of the usurped rights of his people, much as he appreciates anything that eases the hardships they have to endure, the onlooker becomes impatient, for the removal of this tiny flaw in the island paradise isn't going to be all that simple!

9

The Pan Handle

'When in doubt take to the road –'

'The nice thing about this island,' said Kennie, 'is that each place is completely different from the other. Take the Karpas for instance . . .'

'The Karpas? That's the thin point that way?' I pointed to the east.

My companion nodded. 'If it's peace and quiet you want – well! And the people are *marvellous*, so different too. The Crusaders left little souvenirs all over the Karpas you know!' he laughed, throwing a tiny leg of the *ambelopoulia* over his left shoulder.

I had to admit that my companion looked picturesque as he sat picking at the various dishes which made up our *meze*. The well-cut trousers were the same colour as his amethyst eyes, and the open shirt was just one tone darker than the lanky eucalyptus trees that screened us from the beach below.

We were sitting in an open-air restaurant, sipping white wine. Before us was a super *meze*; dishes with nuts, black olives, cucumber cut in long strips, artichoke hearts, grilled octopus, lettuce and tomato, little grilled meat balls, and three kinds of cheeses. I had refused the little *ambelopoulia* – the sparrow-like bird pickled in wine – although my companion assured me they were *delicious*. From the veranda came fine smells from our kebab sizzling on the spit.

'And what's more, darling,' he said, touching my arm, 'the Karpas will set you up – absolutely. Take uncle's word for it!'

'Well, I hope so,' I said, for a bad bout of Asian 'flu had left me with unpleasant side-effects, aggravated by having taken antibiotics for the first time in my life.

We had not long finished the wine and the sweet Turkish coffee, when the expedition was planned.

''Bye Maria!' Kennie called to the proprietor's young wife,

The young shepherd

Sardine catch at Vasilas

Nancy at a United Nations field camp

The author outside the United Nations Headquarters, Nicosia

'marvellous meal, *thank you*! The best food in Cyprus,' he said to me as we climbed into the Land-Rover. 'Why she hasn't been snapped up by someone from London, I can't think.'

'Perhaps she prefers to stay with her husband,' I suggested.

'But that's just it, darling, she works like a black for *nothing*, whilst back in London I could get her a huge salary.' He slammed the door. 'Women puzzle me,' he admitted.

Next morning I put my sleeping bag and kitchen box, together with a few clothes in the back of the Land-Rover. I said goodbye to my hostess and the animals, and taking my aching bones, badly affected eyes and uncertain tummy – all after-effects of the Asian 'flu – I headed towards the Karpas.

This narrow strip was known to the ancients as 'The Deer's Tail' and the moderns call it 'The Pan Handle' which is just what it looks like. It runs for forty miles from the Kyrenia Range to Cape Andreas and is quite different from the rest of the island. Most of the land is agricultural with some small forests and there are far fewer people living here. Until recently, when the roads were improved, very little was known of the area and there are not many facilities for visitors, although more and more campers are finding their way to the beaches and coves along the coast.

I drove along the ridge of the range and at the very end, from the heights of Kantara Castle the whole of the Karpas tapered off below me, like a giant map. There are smaller hills and a long plateau but the area gives the impression of wide-open countryside, and this is accentuated by the scarcity of villages.

Far below me was Komi Kebir, a mixed town of Turks and Greeks, and the U.N. have not found it necessary to patrol farther east than this point, although there are several villages which are entirely Turkish. I dropped down into the town and found the U.N. Swedish contingent stationed in a large school building with its own swimming pool. The bronzed soldiers lay about sun-bathing and it looked more like a first-class hotel than army headquarters. All they lacked obviously was female company.

The road wandered from one side of the narrowing peninsula to the other and climbed to a low plateau already gold with ripening crops. Occasionally a road led to a sandy beach and just before the town of Koma tou Yailou I turned right to a fishing cove of the same name. There was a semi-circle of rock with a small jetty and white sand. On shore was a small café and an old carob warehouse. Fishing nets hanging from a frame to dry made a nice splash of colour for in the Karpas they are a distinctive *vieux rose*. A young fisherman was repairing part of the nets, watched by his girl. They were getting married quite soon and had already built their own bungalow together, as Cypriot couples do. Generally the boy provides the ground and the girl's people the house. Most of these bungalows have an unfinished appearance for the iron joists which run up from the foundations protrude above the walls in readiness for another storey when the family increases. This unfinished state also absolves them from paying rates. They told me a lemon tree had already been planted for it is the first thing most people do once the land has been bought.

Once a couple have officially become engaged they live together and it is a terrible crime for the boy to break off the engagement. Legal action often follows but nothing can compensate the girl for having lost her virginity.

The earth had changed to a rich red loam that contrasted with the dark green of the carob trees. Grass grew from the flat roofs of the few farmhouses along the road. There was already a sense of space and the pace was slower; not the artificial stagnation of the Turkish enclaves, but of smaller populations and of farmers.

The main road runs through Leonarisso where one of the biggest fairs in the island is held in October, and I turned off to Lythrangomi here, in search of the Church of the Blessed Virgin Mary, Kanakaria, which is probably the most important church in the Karpas. It stands beside the road and forms a court with other buildings that were a monastery at one time. Now they are used by a farmer who lives in part and uses the rest as a barn. The church dates from the fifth century when it was a timber-roofed basilica, but it has been re-built and remodelled many times over the centuries.

I passed through an arch in an old stone wall that was crumbling away. The domed silhouette of the church against the blue sky was very beautiful. The church was locked and I rang a bell hanging near by. After a few minutes a large woman came round the side of the building holding the keys in her hand. She wore a black dress and a scarf covered her grey hair. Her dark eyes were intelligent and friendly, and although she spoke no English, she was obviously pleased by the diversion of a visitor.

Many of the churches are locked and in some cases the key will be at the nearest village. If the caretaker is a farmer who is away in the fields, a small boy is sent to fetch him.

The woman opened the low door and let me in. The church has been added to over the years and now has three naves, each with a semi-circular apse. The central one is part of the early Byzantine basilica. The main interest in the church is the mosaic of the Virgin and Child with the Archangels in attendance. It is in typical 'Cypriot' style and the figures are surrounded by an aura of deep blue, which signifies the sublime power. There is no documentary evidence which makes it possible to place the exact date of the mosaic, although the style is similar to some sixth-century ones in Ravenna. The Christ Child remains intact but part of the Virgin and most of the archangels have been destroyed and this is due to the belief that the cubes of the mosaic are a cure for skin diseases.

A Turkish invader is supposed to have struck the picture of the Virgin Mary and was immediately covered with blood from the wound he had made; and the spring called *plytirka* is the place where he washed his hands.

We came out into the sunlight again and the woman locked the door behind us and came down to the Land-Rover with me. She thanked me profusely for the money I gave her and seemed delighted. When I called to see the mosaic again on my return journey, she would take nothing and greeted me as a friend.

The two main towns in the Karpas are Yialousa and the capital Ritzokarpasia, which is more than two thirds of the way along the Pan Handle. Neither town is very large and the Karpasians treat Famagusta as their nearest big town. Yialousa is near the north coast and has a narrow winding main street with few shops, an inferior hotel and the usual cafés.

Farmers' towns have much in common anywhere in the

world and the accent is mainly on the necessities of life and there is not the clutter of the cities.

After leaving Yialousa the road continued for fourteen miles along the north coast. It was wild scrubland country with bushes and low trees that ran to the shore. At odd places the scrub had been cleared on flat ground and made ready for the farmers to plant their summer melons. There was always a small building with a flat roof near by, where the family sleep when the melons are ripening.

Right on the rocky sea-shore there was the tiny chapel of Ayios Thyrsos which is built into the side of the cliff and almost in the sea. Below it and reached through a small hole in the chapel is an underground well. An old man with a suppurating sore on his leg emerged as I arrived. He had been bathing his leg. Now, he assured me, the sore would disappear. I suggested a doctor might do the job quicker but he shrugged his bony shoulders. Was it a matter of money or was he firmly convinced of the saint's powers?

Ritzokarpasia spreads out over a large area for the people like to build with space around them which makes them unique in the island for most Cypriots prefer to build close together, and privacy is not a thing they covet as we do. The main road runs straight along the side of a wide shallow basin and stops at a cluster of glaring white buildings. There is a local co-op, a row of small shops, a couple of cafés and a men's club, whilst on a lower level to the south is a barn-like building which is the market. Near the shops is the white Church of St Synesios with a high square campanile. The original structure was twelfth century but it has been enlarged and altered, with no great improvement. In the Middle Ages it was the cathedral of the Orthodox See, and the choice of such a remote spot for the Bishop of Famagusta to live, came about in 1222 when the legate Pelagius was sent to Cyprus to try and ease the tension caused by the presence of so many bishops and clergy of the Western and Eastern churches living in this close proximity. Pelagius sanctioned the presence of the four Orthodox bishops but arranged for each to take up residence as far as possible from the old See! The Bishop of Nicosia was sent to the Forest Range; the Bishop of Limassol to Lefkara on the southern slopes of the mountains; the Bishop of Paphos to Arsos in the western hills; and the Bishop of Famagusta – to the Pan Handle.

I climbed the steps leading to the row of shops and the post office; and in the general store I inquired about the hotel. The old man regarded me sternly.

'It is closed,' he said, glancing at the clock, 'come back after he has had his afternoon nap.'

Life is easy in Ritzokarpasia.

10

The Saint of Philon

Some ventures, having the element of luck, move with ease from the very start. Or was it just that the Karpas works wonders as Kennie had said?

I left the store and moved out into the bright sunlight. To my left a signpost to Ayios Philon pointed to a steep track which climbed behind the town. It ran across the narrow escarpment and passed many houses, where roses grew to extreme proportions; and then ran under a house which straddled the road. Ahead was the white church of the Holy Trinity with a stone lion keeping guard on a low wall. Beyond were fields enclosed by large, finely cut stones which in all probability had been taken from the ancient mole in the old harbour below. The escarpment dropped away suddenly and the whole of the northern coastline spread out. The only buildings in sight lay near the water's edge where a small cluster of huts and palms were grouped round the ruins of the Church of Ayios Philon; and this is all that is left of the ancient city of Karpasia which, legend has it, was founded by Pygmalion, King of Cyprus, and was in its time as important as Salamis.

Two vast moles, one nearly four hundred feet long, protect the small inlet and they were made of large cut stones that were carefully placed and clamped together with metal. Now a row of fishermen's rooms with a veranda in front overlook the eastern mole, and on the veranda lines of the pink fishing nets were hanging to dry. A low building with a large terrace, fenced against the harbour's drop was the local café with the old church and the palms near by. Another building with precarious wooden stairs running along the outside wall to the floor above, was used by the owner of the café.

I moved from the terrace into the café which had a high bar with a large refrigerator behind it and on the walls were shelves holding rows of Cyprus brandy. A cage-like structure was used for hanging meat and game, and beyond was a large grid for cooking. In the café were a few tables and dozens of chairs both here and on the terrace, for a Cypriot needs five chairs when he sits to have a cup of coffee; one to sit on and one for each of his arms and legs. It was clean but unadorned and with the unmistakable atmosphere of a place successful in its own field; an atmosphere any café-goer or gourmet recognizes at once.

Pol (or Paul) the proprietor sat at a table peeling potatoes. He was a quiet little man with kind and honest eyes. After giving me a cup of coffee, he continued with his job and chatted in excellent English. His wife had recently broken her leg and was in bed in the building opposite and this was why *he* was peeling the potatoes. There were three boys and a girl and the whole family had been in England where he ran a restaurant. So it wasn't by chance that he is one of the best cooks in Cyprus.

'It was the weather,' he said, 'my eldest boy was sick for the sun. So of course we came back.'

As he talked I was looking out along the empty coastline and listening to the waves and the gulls. 'Is there anywhere I could stay down here?' I asked suddenly.

'Here? Oh, you could use one of the fishermen's huts. That is if you have a camp bed,' he added.

'And for food?'

'I'll cook anything you need.'

And so it was settled. The fishermen returned in the late afternoon. They used the rooms mainly for their gear and now they cleaned out one of them, sweeping and washing the floor in an adequate manner. They gave me a long table and about a dozen chairs and moved the nets to the far end of the veranda. They were kindly men, amusing and friendly and with many tales in the way of fishermen the world over. Some of them came from Famagusta and followed the catches around the coast with the seasons. Except for mullet, fish isn't very plentiful and when lobsters were caught they rarely bothered to sell though the prices were high, for they were a delicacy to keep for their families or to be given away as special gifts.

I set up my camp bed with the sleeping bag on top. On the large table I put my few possessions and filled the two-gallon can with water from a natural spring that came out of the bank below Pol's terrace. Later I bought a large blue plastic basin from the co-op in the town at far less than I'd have to pay in London. During the night there was no sound except the lapping of the waves; and the sunrises and sunsets were such that even Pol's small boys remarked on them.

Beyond the harbour the long sandy beach was completely isolated during the week and it was possible to bathe in the nude, although week-ends brought a few trippers who had strayed from the main road. In the evening, however, the café came to life as the villagers arrived to have coffee or brandy, and some brought their own meat for Pol to cook. He supplied chips and a salad with a dressing that would be the envy of any Paris chef. I soon learnt that brandy was ordered by the half or full bottle and not by the nip, but as the cost was roughly nine shillings a bottle, it was no great hardship.

Mrs Pol held court in a large iron bedstead on the ground floor of the other building and tried to keep some sort of discipline over her high-spirited brood. She was nicely plump with the lovely eyes of Cypriot women. Yes, she told me, she missed many things that life in England had given her, but our bad weather entirely discounted all the good points. As well as the extra work thrown on Pol's shoulders by his wife's accident, he missed her presence in the café.

'It is good to have her here,' he told me, 'nobody uses a bad word when she is around.'

When he was coping with the children or taking food to his wife, customers served themselves, going behind the bar and delving into the refrigerator. If a stranger arrived he would be given a drink by a regular to keep him happy until Pol returned.

Officialdom caught up with us one day. I arrived back from a swim to find two well-set-up gentlemen organizing the clearance of all the rooms, but mine. Now they were being swept and washed, and new padlocks were put on each door. The huts, it seemed, were owned by the authorities which really meant the church and could be used by visiting 'persons' such as myself though I was the first to avail myself of the service. Having heard of my arrival the gentlemen had come down to see that I was not only comfortable but clean and suitably padlocked. One of the rooms was full of Pol's feast day surplus tables and chairs and these were now stacked on the rocky ground near by. Pol stood watching the procedure stolidly and without comment.

'We can move you into one of the clean rooms now,' said the spokesman to me, 'and it has a good new padlock.'

I had never contemplated using the old padlock on my door and I assured him that my room was not only perfectly clean and adequately padlocked, but there was nothing whatever that I desired.

Finally they left us, after having padlocked the remaining doors and leaving Pol's furniture still on the rocky ground. I felt guilty that my presence had brought all this to light. We circled the large pile and went in for a cup of coffee.

'I shall write to Makarios,' Pol said at last.

'Archbishop Makarios?'

'Yes. I'll tell him I just must have somewhere to put my chairs. How otherwise can I live? He'll soon fix it.'

'Will he really do something, do you think?' I asked, seeing myself becoming involved in an island-wide issue.

'Of course!' Pol regarded me with surprise, 'he will understand about my chairs. How does he think I can continue to serve people – *without* chairs? And here they will be ruined in the rain. . . .'

'But it never rains. . . .'

'Perhaps it will. I shall explain and you can help me compile the letter.' I groaned.

I was thankful when a key was found to fit one of the padlocks and the offending chairs were put away out of sight. It was the first of many such threats to elicit the help of the Archbishop, although few ever got past the talking stage. He is undoubtedly a father figure to them all and could, they believe, by the raising of his hand put everything right.

Each evening I went over to the café where it was impossible to eat alone, and often difficult to pay for my own meal. There was always someone amongst the gathering who would try, if only surreptitiously, to pay the bill. It is not for nothing that the word *xenos* means both stranger and guest. Pol always produced something for me even though I seldom brought my own meat. It would be freshly grilled chops, liver, kidneys or crisp fried mullet. Where it came from, I never inquired! Pol's catering arrangements worked very well, for he could serve as many as three to four hundred meals during feast days and holidays, but there was no waste if the weather was bad for he kept no perishable stocks except lettuce.

There were many nightly regulars; a local town counsellor farmer, an impressive figure who drank the prescribed amount of brandy and left punctually at nine each night; two old farmers who sat side by side, joining in the conversation but who were never seen speaking to each other; sometimes when the fishermen were not going out they joined the shepherds for a night of conviviality. The flute-playing shepherd Varnavas was a great favourite, he was young and as pixilated as his goats who followed his plaintive tunes all over the plain. Pavlos, the deaf-mute was a fisherman; he had red curly hair and wide innocent eyes, and we all carried on 'conversations' in animated mime. I never really knew how it was he conveyed to me that an Englishman came to Philon most weekends and stayed in the rooms above Pol's place.

Bill Cowell arrived at the weekend. He worked at the British High Commission in Nicosia. He was stocky and strong with close-cropped hair, a beard, an independent air, and was a great favourite with the locals. He had furnished the room above Pol's quarters with a bed, table and chairs, and a cylinder gas cooker.

'I found this spot about two years ago,' he said, 'there's not much to do but swim and laze about, but it's great to get away from Nicosia.'

It said much for his good humour and kindliness that he didn't resent my having invaded his *shangri-la*.

'You'll be interested in all the old bits around here,' he said, 'must let me take you along. I know them all – rock-cut tombs in the cliffs of Tsambres on the other side of the beach; what's left of Aphendrika, *the* oldest city they say. It's about six miles along the coast to the east – and of course St Andreas up near the tip – he looks after them all.'

Bill had a fast open M.G. sports model and we set off one morning for the Monastery of St Andreas. It is at the very end of the main road four miles from the tip of the island. The road leaves Ritzokarpasia and crosses to the south coast where we passed the humped rocks of Khelones, and a series of sandy beaches already showing signs of being 'discovered' with small cafés and parking space. The road climbs to Galounopetra Point where there is a spectacular view of the five-mile sweep of pink sand below.

The Monastery has become a hostel for pilgrims and a resident priest looks after them, with the help of those who have been cured or helped by the miracle-working icon of St Andreas. The buildings form a vast square and thousands of pilgrims trek here each year, staying in the rooms or camping in the open. They bring offerings of every description and also wax effigies of the person who is seeking a cure. On the rocky shore is the small fifteenth-century Gothic Chapel which stands over two springs. Here, it is believed, is the spot where St Andrew first set foot on the island. Behind the chapel is a modern and rather ugly church that is of little interest except for the icon which is covered with silver gilt. A curtain hangs over the whole thing and on it are offerings in silver that represent eyes, legs, arms and fingers, or any portion of the body that the sick person wishes to have cured. Along the west wall are the grotesque wax effigies of all sizes, which have either been sent or brought by those wishing to be cured. These pallid figures with their staring eyes give the place an eerie atmosphere.

St Andrew is the favourite saint in these parts and legend has it that he was passing the cape by ship when they ran out of water. He suggested to the one-eyed captain that he put ashore for supplies, which he did reluctantly, for he did not expect to find water in such an arid area. But the springs were found near the waterside and when the water was taken aboard the captain's sight was restored. Such was his gratitude that on his next voyage the captain erected a shrine near the spring and put an icon of the Saint inside.

It is firmly believed that St Andrew cures the sick, especially the blind, and also protects those who travel by sea. Gunnis reports having met a child in 1935 whose sight was restored as soon as he crossed the threshold of the church.

'Legends?' we queried as we moved round the strange church and listened to the waves beating against the small chapel. Whose to know? And where does the power of faith begin and finish?

No miracles however could help the tyrant Emperor Isaac Comnenus, for it was here he finally surrendered to Richard Coeur de Lion in 1191, having failed to find a ship to take him to Syria.

We bumped over the road to the very tip of the island where on a spectacular rise of rocks called Castras, the Temple of Aphrodite Acraea once stood. Nothing remains of it now, although the ground was covered with anemones and small wild flowers of every description. Thousands of birds, resting on their way north, flew around us. The spot is perpetually windswept and the waters far below us were so clear we could see the ocean bed. Separated by nothing more than a step of crystal clear water is the rock of Klides whose rocky surface was also alive with birds. It was a wild lively scene that has probably changed little since Aphrodite's time – except that the Temple and the Altar have gone; and so have the maidens who gathered here, but few places can have been more spectacular as a setting for the sacrifice to their goddess Aphrodite.

Sometimes we came across little churches or chapels tucked away in unexpected places, almost underground, in a field or a cave and half in the sea. Not far from Philon is the small thirteenth-century Chapel of St Mavra and its dome of red tiles rose above a field of corn. One solitary candle illuminated the wall-painting of St Demetrius astride a white horse, and on the floor were the remains of the original mosaic. We missed a vicious-looking snake by inches as we inspected the thin red Romanesque bricks that form a chevron pattern over the door.

There are many saints that are seldom heard of outside the island. St Mavra it is believed was a niece of St Barnabas and she married St Timothy, although Cypriots will tell you that as a girl she wished to enter the convent but her father forced her to marry a wealthy merchant. During the wedding celebrations she fled and when her absence was noticed her father and the bridegroom set off after her. When they finally caught up with the young bride she had reached the edge of a cliff where she prayed desperately to the Madonna to save her, beating her hands on the bare rock as she did so; whereupon the Virgin caused the rock to open and the young girl disappeared inside. When the bridegroom tried to follow, a spring of water issued from the crevice which can be seen even today.

As we left the Chapel of St Mavra and crossed the corn field, a young woman came towards us from a house near by. In her hand were three roses which she smilingly gave me. The presentation had a slight air of benediction.

'Funny, how they always do that,' said Bill.

'Give flowers? Yes, the women do it all the time,' I said. Is it after all, an echo of the spring worship of the Goddess Aphrodite?

The still quiet days of the Karpas made exploring and sight-seeing very pleasant. About two miles along the main road reaching Ritzokarpasia is a turning to the right that leads to the Monastery of the Blessed Virgin Mary. It belongs to the Monastery of St Katherine of Sinai. The Monastery is derelict now but the sixteenth-century church is open and well cared for. The buildings stand alone in a forest of olive and carob trees, with no sign of habitation in any direction. There is an atmosphere of departed activity. The church had been whitewashed inside and out, and any frescoes there may have been are completely obliterated. The two naves are divided by arches which are carried on thick rounded pillars that are completely unadorned. It has the austere whiteness of a mosque. We knew the church had three small icons of the sixteenth century but they were locked away and the place was completely deserted. The sunlight fell sharply on the archway of the south door which is decorated with perfect dog-tooth moulding.

Originally all churches were built standing due east and west with the altar to the east so that one faces the rising sun. The entrance to the church was to the west through the porch and with the pulpit on the north wall. Stalls are built against the walls and the Bishop's throne, with a wooden canopy, stands by the south wall. There is a gallery for women and children, and the ornate iconostasis or screen which divides the sanctuary from the congregation, is the focal point of the church. It is generally raised above the floor of the nave. Behind is the Holy Table with the Vestry one side and the altar of prothesis on the other. The Holy Table is mounted and is made of wood.

Sometimes in Cyprus large stone columns that have been taken from an ancient ruin are used for the purpose.

The icons are the most important possession in the church and they hang on the iconostasis. Those of the Redeemer and the Madonna are given place of honour. Also, ones of St John the Baptist, the Archangel Michael, and the saint to whom the church is dedicated, though they are not placed in any particular order and are often changed. Also today one finds the photograph of a local hero who died during the EOKA uprising – the twentieth-century saint.

The swimming from the deserted beach is wonderful; and all kinds of things are washed up on the sand, old wooden wheels, pieces of palm trunks smooth and silver-grey, bits of wrecks; and in the rock pools are tiny fish and crabs. It was fine wandering round with Pol's dog at my heels, or exploring the rock tombs near by that are empty now except at night when the goats are hemmed in with bracken. Naturally in such a place, the bad effects of the Asian 'flu disappeared.

There are a few Turkish Cypriot villages along the Pan Handle but the Karpasians are more tolerant towards them; which is just as well for they are surrounded and isolated.

Galinoporni lies near the south coast and the road to it runs past Kanakaria Church and the village of Ayios Symeon which is also Turkish. A more direct approach is to go due south from Ritzokarpasia, across stubbly forest land which is completely deserted. The road peters out several times and the way is not possible except by Land-Rover. The track then becomes more defined as it runs out below the village where there is a football ground. Galinoporni clings to the cliff face above, its white houses, piled one above the other, and eucalyptus trees struggle to keep a grip. My appearance disrupted a game for a group of young men were playing as I drew up. They crowded round, surprised at my arrival 'from the opposite direction'.

Finally I made a precarious ascent and came to a ledged square where there was a small empty café, but soon a police officer arrived who spoke excellent English. He had the easy manner of so many Cypriot officials and was delighted to speak English again.

'I used to speak it all the time' he said, 'but now I have no practice whatsoever.'

The area is noted for the many large caves and tombs that are cut in the cliff sides. We climbed farther to inspect one which is below a ledge and almost impossible to reach. The largest is near Ayios Symeon and is set half way up the cliff side. Tombs have been dug to a depth of eighty-five feet. It was used as a communal burial place; today it can make an excellent air raid shelter.

The largest Turkish Cypriot village in the area is Galatia which lies in the centre of the Karpas and not far from the main road. It stands on a flat plateau and has a magnificent view of the plain below. It is a clean, rather bare village with few trees, and free from clutter, due no doubt to the years when nothing but the bare necessities were allowed in. A large white mosque with a slender minaret stands apart and in the square are a couple of cafés, and a restaurant where several men were having their lunch. I joined them for an excellent meal which was cooking in a large pan outside the restaurant and we helped ourselves. We ate the peppery goulash-type dish with coarse bread. It was very good. None of the men spoke English but we managed with gestures and after all, appreciation of one's food brings all men together.

Plantanisso, the other village, is very different. It lies at the end of a forgotten valley, over a high hill from the north coast. You could be going back some hundreds of years as you drive along the valley and up into the village which is small and primitive; beautiful in a hard stark way – and rather frightened. They let me come – and go – but they watched me with wary eyes.

The best parties just grow – they evolve and are never pre-arranged. Some are remembered more vividly than others and for a long time; a pre-New Year party in Helsinki, a mid-day one in Hong Kong, and another that went on for two days following the arrival of a caravan in Southern Arabia. Now, we were sitting in the bright light of the Tilley lamps and the air was full of conviviality, for Pol's café needs no soft lights or music to create the right atmosphere. I was pleasantly drowsy but with the glorious sense of well being that comes from too much strong sea air. Pavlos and I had spent all afternoon in a skiff, following the coast almost as far as Cape Andreas, and we had called in at a few small inlets. I was still wondering just how he had been able to convey so many tales and things of interest to me *en route*. Now he sat across the room, his bright red hair gleaming and he was giving me, from time to time, such warm grins of friendship that the world at this moment was a truly safe and pleasant place.

On our table were plates of tiny grilled chops, barbounia the fresh fried mullet, a lobster and mountains of chips. Brandy bottles formed an amber fresco and amongst it all stood a bottle of 'Vat 69'. This touch of sophistication belonged to an elderly local man who had returned from England on a visit. There was no doubt he had been most successful overseas, and now as a widower he had returned to find another wife.

Varnavas the shepherd slid into the chair beside me, his bright eyes taking in everything. Had the playing of the flute made him look so much of a faun, I wondered? Bill moved from table to table, for he knew everyone. Pol slipped a dish of freshly grilled little chops in front of me – they were delicious.

'He's very rich,' said Pol, nodding conspiringly towards the returned prodigal.

'No good, Pol,' I said, 'I like my "lonely" life.'

'Perhaps you are right.'

What is it that turns every married person into a matchmaker?

Our prodigal had a fund of *risqué* stories that were out of place but the great good humour of the gathering swept over them. Now we were eating kephalotiri and salad, it is a Gruyère type of cheese delicious with chunks of bread. Bill had bought some haloumi from the market. It is half cheese – half sweet which has its origins in Turkey, but is eaten by both sections of the community.

'Come on, Varnavas, Pavlos, Bill . . . ' Tables were pushed back and the dancing began. It is the men who dance in Cyprus sometimes using a vigorous step curiously like a Russian one and another, far more erotic, that I had last seen in Black Africa. There was the *Karfoilarnos* with other variations called

Tobacco planting in the Karpas

The cafe, Ayios Philon, Karpas

St Katherine's Church, Karpas

Protos and *Deftnos*. As one dancer fell out another took his place and there was a curious affinity, and an erotic exchange of emotions between the couples as they faced each other. Sometimes a lone dancer took the floor to give us the *Syrtos* when he was hailed and clapped with great enthusiasm. The dances are handed down but each village has its own variation. The steady beat went on and the whole café vibrated with the happy flushed crowd. The brandy bottles shook precariously on the shelf and on the tables and Pol, his dark eyes amused and alight, watched from behind his high bar. Later there were feats of strength and one boy picked up a square table complete with glasses in his teeth and slowly danced around the room.

The prodigal, affected earlier than the others by the strong liquor, had long since departed; and later when I made my way to the fishermen's huts the beat of the dancers followed me down. It was quiet here, except for the distant beat, the sea was calm – and the bright moon gave it a sheen.

Narnavas and his companions were departing now, and the tune of the flute became fainter and fainter as they made their way across the plain. And then there was no more sound and the light went out in the café and I heard Pol humming lightly to himself as he walked past the old ruined church, on his way to the other building. Out on the rocks the water made a small curling sound – and there was nothing else.

Few people knew the exact whereabouts of Aphendrika which, it is believed, was the ancient city of Urania. It lay somewhere east of Ayios Philon in that pocket not touched by the main road to Cape Andreas. The best way to get there, everyone agreed, was to go by boat or to walk.

'Let's see how far we can get with the Land-Rover,' said Bill and we set out one morning going due east and keeping to the edges of the fields. Several low stone walls forced us towards the shore so that we had to retrace our steps many times, but finally a narrow but straight track led us past a small hut where a woman and two children stood watching us. The woman nodded at our inquiry, pointing ahead and when I offered the children some sweets, they had to be urged by their mother before they would come near. The hut stood on bare rock and the ground was entirely uncultivated.

Aphendrika has never been excavated and the ruins cover a large area, from the harbour which is silted up to the remains of three churches overlooked by the citadel, that are a mile inland and alongside the track we were on.

The citadel is extraordinary for the whole of the large foundation and part of the walls have been chiselled out of the living rock. To keep the floor level, parts of the walls where the stone had been higher were carved as deep as four feet and at one end the natural stone remains untouched beyond the structure. The masonry which completed the building has gone, but the whole solid foundation and plan remains indestructible and is fascinating to trace.

Below it is the Church of the Blessed Virgin Mary Chrysiotissa that was built in the twelfth century. The outer walls measure seventy-five feet long, but it was destroyed, either by earthquake or vandals and in the fourteenth century another smaller church was built within its walls. This pleasant little church is in a good state of preservation having been protected by the outer one; but little remains of the other two churches. One, in the domed Byzantine style has half the structure completely gone and the other has nothing but a portion of the aisle and part of the nave. The whole area is so completely overgrown that soon they will disappear altogether. There are rumours of a plan to open up this remote part by building a holiday village near the old city. Who knows, if we should return a good sealed road might bring us here in a matter of minutes?

There was great excitement in Ayios Philon as Easter drew near, for not only is it a great celebration everywhere in the island but in Ritzokarpasia the festivities go on for many days, culminating in a fair which brings many people into the town. Merchants arrive and set up stalls in the area surrounding the Church of St Synesios.

Despite Mrs Pol still being in bed, there were many preparations in the family. There was the Easter Cake made of cheese, eggs and sultanas, and Pol was busy boiling some eggs in different colours for the children. Each family buys and kills a lamb or sheep, and on the day of the burial of Christ the young girls of the village build a grave of flowers in the church and the icon is laid upon it.

Pol had a lot on his mind for if the weather was good on Sunday he would have crowds of people from all over the island, on the other hand if it was bad . . . He charged a shilling each to cook the food they brought and they paid extra for the vegetables and wine.

'If the weather is bad,' he said, 'it will be a pity for these feast days are the ones that bring in good money. However . . .' he shrugged and went on colouring the eggs with seaweed gathered from the rocks below.

I laughed. 'You don't seem over worried, Pol,' I said and looked at the large pile of lettuces.

'Oh,' he said glancing towards the ruins of the church, 'it will be all right, I'm sure. *He'll* see to that.'

'He? And who is "he"?' I asked.

'Philon, he always looks after us.'

'Does he now? Well, I must say it's convenient having a saint right on your very doorstep.'

'It is no good to laugh,' he said. 'Once when I was very ill and could not do any work, I had no *will* to work, he came to me one night and told me to get up. I did – and now look at me. Working like a slave!' he added, laughing.

'Oh, Pol, you're a happy man!' I said.

'I have my troubles,' but his grin belied the remark.

Towards midnight on Easter Saturday we made our way to the church where a long sermon was in progress. The church was crowded and the congregation spilled out into the court so that it was quite difficult to move around. Already some of the stalls had been erected and those selling sweets were doing a good trade. There were many young people amongst the crowd who had come from the cities to be with their parents for the holiday, and one young man was brought along to be introduced for he spoke perfect French and had been living for some time in France. The inside of the church was brilliant with lights and candles and the long sermon continued. Suddenly the lights went out in the church and all around us, leaving only the mellow glow from the candles. In many other parts of the island where tensions were running high, this could have caused panic, but the priest continued his sermon until the fault was corrected and the lights came on again. Finally there was a stir in the church, a general movement and the priest having resurrected the Icon, started the procession that moved slowly round the church and out through the high doors into the court. Slowly they circled the church and the whole congregation followed, each murmuring 'Christ is Risen'. Everyone greeted us in this way, and we replied 'Christ is Risen'. The murmur went out all over the village, as they finally dispersed; and the flickering candles could be seen moving out and spreading over the shallow town.

Pol's prophesies had been right and it was a fine day. The people crowded into the café and on the terrace in good-tempered disorder and he was cooking far into the night.

'Pol,' I said next morning as we sat amongst the debris sipping coffee. 'You were not paid for all those drinks!' for one of our regulars had been particularly merry and ordering drinks all round, 'he will never remember.'

He shrugged. 'What can you do? He hasn't the money anyway.'

I laughed. 'You'll never get rich!'

'He was *very* happy,' he said with a grin.

If the plans to build a large holiday village with chalets, communal shops and restaurants goes through, lots of people will benefit no doubt, but with its coming will go the world of Pol, Pavlos and the flute-playing shepherd; and the great fraternity.

11

Kokkina

Kokkina is a name that keeps cropping up every time the 'situation' is discussed. It still has an ominous ring, for it is a sensitive spot, a smouldering volcano that can erupt at the first sign of trouble in the island.

The small Turkish enclave lies on the north-west coast and the Greek Cypriots attacked and cut it off just five months after the UNFICYP established themselves on the island in 1964. Immediately, upon this action, there were Turkish air attacks on Greek areas near by and the whole thing was the climax to intensified military preparations on both sides. A month earlier Archbishop Makarios had introduced conscription and General Grivas arrived from Greece to help train the National Guard. As many as 5,000 men were reputed to have arrived from Greece and were spirited away in the night, to the mountains. At the same time it was rumoured that Turkish volunteers from the mainland were arriving with arms near Kokkina at the rate of one hundred a week. The Makarios government instituted an economic blockade of the Turkish areas and stopped supplies of petrol and anything else that could be used for military purposes. He also restricted food supplies from the Turkish Red Crescent despite the fact that almost half the Turkish Cypriot population depended on these for their existence. The Greek attack on Kokkina was aimed at cutting off any illegal supplies that might be filtering through. The new Greek National Guard, armed with twenty-five pounders, mortars and bazookas moved in and two days later, Turkish jet fighters attacked the Greek positions killing or wounding three hundred people and destroying several villages. It certainly looked as though things were getting out of hand.

Immediately the Security Council called for a cease fire, whereupon the Greek Government promised to support Cyprus should there be a Turkish invasion. Finally the Greek Cypriot leaders announced that if the bombing by the Turkish planes did not stop they would invade all the Turkish Cypriot enclaves and little imagination was needed to realize the fate of the population. This threat had effect and the Turkish jet fighters retired. Perhaps also they had made their point, or the fact that Makarios having appealed to Russia and received a promise of help should Cyprus be invaded, influenced the cease fire. The U.S.A. also warned Turkey that neither she nor NATO would support them against Russia should that country intervene.

For the time being the tension relaxed, but Kokkina remains an uneasy spot and at the first sign of any emergency the small enclave closes its 'frontiers' and the coast road is blocked. During these times the only chance of entering the enclave is with an escort from UNFICYP.

Nancy with her usual thoroughness had arranged for us to be accompanied into Kokkina. The U.N. Irish contingent in charge of the area had their headquarters in Xeros, which meant we started the day by having breakfast with as many good-looking and charming Irishmen as you'd hope to meet this side of Donegal. Their headquarters lay on the outskirts of the town, and we set off with Captain Murphy in my Land-Rover. We passed the jetty where the copper, mined by the American-owned Cyprus Mines Corporation of Skousiotissa, 'Our Lady of the Slag Heaps' is loaded, as it has been since the second millennium B.C. There is little left to see of Soli, which had been a large city founded in 600 B.C., for the most useful stones and blocks were shipped to Port Said and used in the building of the quays there.

We climbed steeply to the headland where the mysterious and spectacular ruins of the Vouni Palace stand. Far below and to the east is the curve of the Bay of Morphou with the ore jetties and around to the west on the far point are the rocks of Petra tou Limniti which, it is said, were hurled against the invading Saracens by the hero Dighenis. Beyond is the wide expanse of sea. The headland and the palace appear to be suspended above the long line of the sea coast and at every turn of the head the view is spectacular.

The date of the palace is set around the fifth century B.C. although no mention is made of it in history, nor of the small township that clung to the steep hillside. Excavations have found no clue to its owner and creator, although because of its magnificent setting and the layout of the palace, with each terrace or hall complementing the view on every side, it would have belonged to a local king or person of importance whose taste for luxury was as pronounced as his love of beauty, as the elaborate baths and hot water systems indicate.

It is not always possible to tell in Cyprus whether ruins were caused by old raiders, recent bombing, earthquakes, or damage caused during the EOKA troubles. We passed a group of wrecked houses as we neared Kokkina which could have been even more recent and inflicted in the 1964 skirmish.

The 'frontier' was set dramatically on a headland between high rocks. A post with a barrier like a barber's pole barred the way and several oil drums painted red stood near by. A young Turkish soldier in grey uniform came out of a small hut that flew the red and white Turkish flag. He inspected our passports and we waited whilst the Colonel in the village, a mile away, was contacted. Finally we dipped down into a deep cove and on the headland beyond was Kokkina backed by red hills that were almost devoid of vegetation. The village consisted of a small group of houses, a football pitch and the familiar conglomeration of tents and shanty buildings recognizable as a refugee camp. We pulled up in front of a low white building beside a bullet-ridden vintage car. The position of the village was very exposed and a perfect target for attack. A group of men watched our approach and a young man who was the local schoolmaster, stepped forward to act as interpreter. He told us the Colonel would be with us immediately and led the way into the white building.

The enclave is completely isolated for the hills beyond are surrounded by Greek-Cypriot territory. Now more supplies are being allowed in by the Greeks but previously the enclave relied almost entirely on the Turkish Red Cross for their food. Smuggling both by sea and land went on but in neither case was it easy. Although things were better the refugee problem remained, for the people did not feel secure enough to return to their own homes in the Greek sector.

The Colonel was a slightly built man with a sallow complexion and a drooping moustache. He wore a green windcheater, grey trousers and a dark felt hat. He looked like a typical mainland Turk. It had surprised everyone that he consented to see us, for even his presence in Kokkina was not always admitted. But he was not unfriendly and studied our questions before answering. The problems of the refugees, of housing and supplies were uppermost. And the final solution? An overwhelming uncertainty. Once again there was the complete barrier of destroyed trust. There seemed no way round this and it would get worse as the two sides never met.

There was little interest in the affairs and troubles of the other enclaves unless they, in some way, affected their own. The Colonel regarded us impersonally.

'We live from day to day,' he said, 'we are not strong enough to take the initiative.'

'Even through friendship?' I asked.

'Friendship?'

'If you had Greek friends, isn't it possible to come back eventually to being on a friendly footing with them?'

'Friendship!' he repeated and suddenly his composure left him. 'Oh God!' and he broke down completely. It is always a shock to see a man cry.

'How?' he asked at last, 'could there ever be any trust? How can I personally forget, when all my family has been killed – almost before my eyes?'

His former air of detachment was not just singleness of purpose. I had seen the same look on an Arab's face whose whole family was killed near him. He was like the branch of a tree, detached and abandoned.

Later we walked through the mud of the refugee quarter. There were many one-room huts, all scrupulously clean despite the lack of water, and low tents that the U.N. Forces had given them. They kept out the rain but little else.

'It is as well,' said our companion, 'that the spring is coming.'

In one small room there was a girl, recently married. She was very young and at the moment radiantly happy. We smiled at each other. As we moved off the schoolteacher looked at me. 'Yes,' he said, 'she's happy. Such things can happen, even here.'

As we drove off I looked back. The small group stood huddled together, watching us, for we had been a diversion, and the slight figure of the Colonel was there also; but isolated – a pace apart.

Monasteries always seemed to me remote and inaccessible places where men of a certain kind lead a life apart, half way between our existence on this earth and the other, and where occasionally pilgrims came seeking re-affirmation of their beliefs, but where women had no existence. I soon learnt that this wasn't so with the monasteries of Cyprus for they are accessible to everyone, men, women, any religion or denomination, and until the Greek–Turkish estrangement Turkish Cypriot women were often seen visiting some miracle-working icon in a monastery. Without doubt the monasteries and religion as a whole are a part of everyday life and are involved in the workings and aims of the community, a fact forcefully brought home during the EOKA uprising when many of the monasteries stored arms for the rebels and gave sanctuary to them as well. It is an odd mixture of reverence and mumbo-jumbo that makes nearly every man touch his penis whenever he sees a priest.

There are so many monasteries on the island, occupied or abandoned, that it would take years to explore them all, but a few stand out above the others, and since early times they have welcomed visitors as they do today. Perhaps the richest and most famous is Kykko which is known all over the Greek Orthodox world, for it houses one of the three icons reputed to have been painted by St Luke that has special sanctity. Kykko also has the distinction, together with that of Makhairas and Ayios Neophytos, of being exempt from the jurisdiction of the diocesan bishop; and the abbot ranks with bishops of the church. A more recent claim to fame is that Archbishop Makarios served his first apprenticeship here.

Previously the monastery owned large and wealthy estates in Russia, Romania and Asia Minor and had a close association with Tsarist Russia, but after the revolution it was forced to depend more on its properties in Cyprus which were also very considerable. The monastery was founded in 1080 after the Byzantine Governor of Cyprus had been cured by the local hermit Isaias, and in gratitude he obtained for him the golden miracle-working icon from the Emperor in Constantinople and Kykko was built to house the precious relic.

Like other Cypriot monasteries it has been destroyed many times by fire. On the second occasion it was re-built by Eleanor of Aragon the wife of Peter the First, for although she belonged to the Latin faith, she had been impressed by the miracles the icon performed and also by its power as a rainmaker. The last fire occurred in 1813 when the buildings and most of the church were completely destroyed, but on all these occasions the icon was saved. The monastery lies in the heart of the Paphos Forest 4,500 feet above the sea. A large tarmaced space has been cleared around the monastery buildings for visitors to park their cars and there are more than seventy guest rooms where both men and women can stay. A collection of assorted buildings form a solid outer wall and they are set around two irregular courtyards. The high entrance cuts through the building into the first court.

A fierce wind was blowing through the trees as I drove up, it made them bend in a 'bowing' gesture towards the monastery and this is regarded with reverence by the pilgrims. It was off-season for tourists and a large corrugated iron stall was boarded up. The monastery looked completely deserted as I walked through the arch into the court whose uncluttered whiteness and sudden quiet were very pleasant. As I turned looking for the church, a cheery little monk came hurrying towards me along the colonnaded gallery. He moved with quick steps and his face radiated good humour and a welcome. Had I come to stay? Ah well . . . then just for a short visit I'd want to see the icon perhaps? And the other things of interest? He led me through the empty court and along a labyrinth of passages and stairs; and when we came to the church he unlocked the door and stepped back for me to enter, carrying on an animated conversation all the time. I was from Australia. Well! He had relations over there – so far away.

It isn't a very impressive little church and the main interest is the famous icon which stands in a handsome shrine of mother-of-pearl and tortoiseshell on a little dais; and the actual painting has a silver-gilt plate cover whilst the whole thing is covered again with a cloth decorated with a figure of the Virgin Mary and edged with seed pearls. There is a tiny hole but nothing really can be seen of the icon and I had been warned of the many terrible and strange things that happened to people who tried to look at it.

In times of drought the icon was taken from the church and placed outside on a high platform facing the direction from where the rain should come. One supposes that if the rain *doesn't* come then the Virgin was displeased about something. A Dutch traveller named Van Bruyn who visited Cyprus towards the end of the seventeenth century tells of this same ceremony being performed against a plague of locusts when, as soon as the icon had been put on the platform, a great number of birds, not unlike plovers, swooped down and ate the locusts.

A bronze arm hangs near the icon, as a warning perhaps, for it is believed that when a Turk tried to light his cigarette at one of the icon's lamps, the outraged Virgin withered the offending arm and turned it into bronze. My companion pointed out a 'saw' of a swordfish which was given to the monastery by a grateful sailor who prayed to the Virgin of Kykko when he was in danger of drowning; and was saved. There are so many of these small relics, kept, one feels, as we might a toy black cat, because to throw away 'good luck' just isn't on.

None of Kykko's other icons can compete with the famous one and there is little else of interest except perhaps a painting by Cornaro the Cretan artist; some Gospels with highly decorated covers, and the numerous boxes of relics from saints and pieces of their bones.

It was fine to be out in the sunlight again and my companion took me along the gallery throwing open one door after the other to show the accommodation for guests. They were all pleasant, plain rooms with thick walls and deep recesses.

'You must come back,' he said, 'and stay. It is very quiet here and peaceful. Now, it is more than peaceful.'

I kept up as best I could for he flitted along the passages at great speed.

'Come!' he said, 'and sign our book.'

He opened another door and I moved into a low vaulted room that could have been a cellar except that there was a bed, a high square affair rather like a ship's bunk. Beyond, arches led to another part of the room, a kind of study where there was a large desk, many books piled in the deep recesses of the windows and a narrow upright sofa with wooden ends.

'Sit down, sit down,' he said, 'what would you like? Some coffee? Some plums?' and he gave me a kiss.

To be fair, it wasn't a very compromising kiss, but I sat down abruptly on the upright sofa, more from surprise than anything else, only to find the little monk had left the room. What, I wondered, do I do now? But he was back almost immediately, coming at a run and with some preserved plums in a saucer.

'Have them,' he said, sitting beside me on the sofa and looking round for more to give me. 'I know, something . . .' and springing up he had disappeared once more.

I had just arranged my cameras, notebook and bag on the seat between me and the rest of the room, as a cautionary barricade, when my host returned with a stick of *soujougo* which is the local sweet rather like tasteless transparent nougat. Taking a penknife from the desk he cut it into thin slices.

'It is good?' he asked in his kindly enthusiastic way. I nodded as I ate my plums, but seemed to be getting primmer and primmer – an elderly spinster on an outing!

'Fine!' I said at last, having finished the plums, 'perhaps I can sign the book now?'

'Of course,' he said, finding it amongst the chaos on the desk, 'but you will come back to stay?' he asked. 'There is much we can show you and many interesting stories to tell.'

'Yes,' I collected my cameras, notebook and bag, 'I shall bring my girl friend with me,' I said.

He came with me to the outer doorway. 'You will forgive me that I am enthusiastic, that I kiss you?' he asked.

I grinned. 'Oh, yes, of course.' He seemed so happy; and who am I to be surprised or upset at other people's customs?

Another of the island's most important monasteries also happens to be exempt from the jurisdiction of the diocesan bishop; it is Makhairas which stands in pine forests on Mount Chioni and has a splendid view looking north across the Mesaoria Plain and was founded in 1200 by a hermit named Nilus. His *Ritual Ordinance* which is written on vellum and kept in the monastery is quite the most quoted and, in many ways, up-to-date piece of literature about the island. Otherwise apart from one of their icons which they believe can work miracles there is little of interest here for the buildings were burnt to the ground at the end of the last century and the monastery has been entirely re-built. Makhairas played a very large part during the EOKA troubles and the monks gave sanctuary to many of the underground fighters. It was here that Gregory Afxentious, who later became a national hero for his work in the cause, was hidden for some time.

There are many more not so famous monasteries all over the island, some large and others so small that a solitary monk will be found living there in the company of a dog and a few chicks. Even the deserted ones have something of interest for in most cases the church belonging to the monastery has been kept up. The search and discovery of many of these took us on fine jaunts all over the island. There was a certain similarity amongst them which I began to recognize just as the various saints were found time and again in their typical poses on the frescoes or icons; St George attacking his dragon, the dog-faced Christopher and St Mamas on his lion and with the lamb in his arms. St Mamas is understandably popular for he objected to paying taxes and got away with it. He lived in a cave near Morphou and after he had protested about the taxes, two soldiers were sent by the Byzantine Ruler to bring him back to Nicosia to be tried. In due course the three set off on foot for the capital and they had not gone far when a lion in pursuit of a small lamb, ran right across their path; whereupon St Mamas held up his hand and the lion stopped dead. The hermit picked up the trembling lamb and obviously thinking of the long trek ahead of him, mounted the wild lion and they all set off once again. When they arrived at the capital, the procession advanced right up to the palace and St Mamas urged the lion ahead so that it climbed the steps and they entered the throne room. The Ruler stared in amazement at the strange sight, but decreed that St Mamas need never pay taxes for the rest of his life. It is little wonder he is seen astride the lion and with the lamb in his arms on so many of the icons and frescoes!

12

The Three Castles

ST HILARION – THE ARROGANT ONE

As a child I loved a large tree in our garden; it was my own private sanctuary and I can remember every branch of it. Other people become attached to views or mountains which they see every day and when I returned to the Little Hut there was a pleasant feeling of recognition as I looked at the long range that backs our plain, and at the three castles of St Hilarion, Buffavento and Kantara that top their peaks.

St Hilarion is the nearest and on a clear morning appears to tower right above us. It is the most important both in size and position and is the story-book castle of all time with its ramparts and smooth green surrounded by crags where the Knights jousted. Small wonder Walt Disney used it as a model for his 'Snow White' castle. Astride the very summit there is a sheer drop to our plain below and from the ramparts it is possible to see across to Turkey and the mountains of Anatolia. On the eastern side, the mountain falls away to a gap in the range which makes the pass from Kyrenia to Nicosia.

The first permanent resident, it is said, was the hermit St Hilarion who came from Egypt in search of solitude and a place to meditate. Settling on this isolated spot he found it occupied by devils who had realized they could not stay with such a pious companion and raised an awful din at his approach. The saint, who was known for his sense of humour, merely remarked that at least he had come to a place where he was welcomed with music. Such a reaction by the intruder was too much for the devils who had no redress and they fled leaving the saint in sole possession. In time he attracted many pilgrims and the foundation of a monastic order followed.

All three mountain castles were fortified against the Arab raiders who attacked the island in the eleventh century and so they, together with Kyrenia Castle, gave a unified protection.

The Lusignans strengthened them further in the thirteenth century and later they carried out many repairs on St Hilarion to make it habitable for the Lusignan Royal Family who used it as a summer retreat.

There was a biting wind when I collected Nancy on the day we decided to visit the castle. It would have been difficult without the Land-Rover for the climb is hard and very long and the castle lies in the Turkish Nicosia enclave. Half way up the mountain is a wooden café where it is necessary to stop for permission to go on. In no time at all a jeep came down from the castle above. The officer inside gave us a quick glance.

'Of course,' he said, 'go right ahead.'

The road climbs all the time and runs across a buff where to the left is the romantic jousting ground surrounded by high cliffs. The road makes a few more giddy turns and runs on to an open space outside the castle walls. A cheerful young Turkish soldier met us and led the way into the lower court which becomes almost perpendicular on the far mountainside. The castle is built on three levels and this lower court is large and open. It was used as accommodation for soldiers and horses, and the stables that form one wall are now used by the soldiers. The deep steps that are cut in the steeply rising ground are broken and overgrown and we climbed bracing ourselves against the cold wind. They led to a vaulted passage which the Lusignans built, that in its turn took us to a small Byzantine church and some royal apartments which were all completely bare. There is a charming little belvedere and terrace with a view that made the steep and cold climb well worth while. A terrace along the northern edge ran past vaulted chambers to the remains of a large water tank, which was very necessary in times of siege. From here there is a sheer drop to the diminutive farmhouses far below and it is probably from this spot that John, Prince of Antioch who was besieged by the Genoese in 1373, had his Bulgarian mercenaries thrown over the parapet. He had been wrongly informed that they were turning against him and fell into the trap, for then he was left without any protection whatsoever.

This was as far as the Turkish soldier would let us go for the

United Nations post near Larnaca

The Mosque, Galatia, Karpas

Klidhes Islands, the tip of the 'Pan Handle', Karpas

special Royal Apartments above were at the moment 'out of bounds' to civilians.

From wherever you look at it, St Hilarion seems to be a living castle that will always be part of the island's changing scene. It is beautiful, with a sense of ironic challenge about its great walls; in keeping perhaps is the fact that when the Turkish Cypriots fought off the attacks by the Greek Cypriots in 1964, the castle was held by a tiny group of boys none of whom was over sixteen!

BUFFAVENTO – THE SAD ONE

Not so the sad Buffavento – 'blown by the wind' – which until recently few people felt strong enough to visit. Its position is higher than both the other castles and it becomes lost in the jumble of mountain peaks that lie east between St Hilarion and Kantara. Now a road has been built a little farther up the mountain and a lot of debris has been cleared from the remaining path and rails put at dangerous sections.

The Greeks called the castle Koutsouvendis, or the Castle of a Hundred and One Houses, no doubt because of the many rooms that were built one above the other on the mountainside and over the summit. It is believed that the person who discovers and passes through the door of the Hundred-and-First Room will disappear for ever into an enchanted garden.

It is surprising how little is known of the castle's early history and all that is left of the crumbling walls give no clue to the date of the original structure, nor why the medieval chronicles referred to it as the 'Castle of the Lion'. It was certainly standing when Richard Coeur de Lion captured the island in 1191, for it was from here that Isaac Comnenus's daughter surrendered to the King, putting herself and the castle at his mercy, an act which helped him greatly in his capture of the other fortresses and towns.

This energetic young person became Lady-in-Waiting to Queen Berengaria and went with her to Acre. Later, one of the conditions made by the German Emperor Henry VI for the release of Richard was that the girl should be released, as she was a relative of his. She made an unsuccessful marriage with Raymond VI Count of Toulouse, and in 1202 married for the second time a French Knight, a relative of Baldwin, Count of Flanders. Together they returned to Cyprus to claim the crown, but the Lusignan King Amaury informed them that unless they left the island he would have them executed.

Even on my earlier visit to the island I had been lackadaisical about arranging a visit to Buffavento and it was Kennie who finally organized the excursion.

'I *want* to see it, darling!' he said, 'and it's only that big Land-Rover of yours that'll get us there.' He was sitting in the garden nursing Biscuit our blonde cat. 'See how she matches my trousers?'

'That's why you picked her up.'

'Beast!'

'And why do you want to go to Buffavento especially? I would have thought it was the last place you'd visit.'

'All those tragedies and horrors, I love them. That clever and mad King Peter the First in thirteen hundred and something or other, imprisoned his best friend and left him to die of starvation.'

'Well, there won't be much to show . . . '

'Killed, he was later. Hoist with his own petard so to speak – and by a lot of nobles too.'

'But I don't think that happened in the castle.'

'Doesn't matter. And then what about those brothers Montolif, very well known they were, imprisoned up there by James the First and one of them escaped down that awful cliff only to be caught in Kyrenia. Kyrenia of all places! And even then, he had them both beheaded. Mean! You can't tell me some of it doesn't *stick*.'

'Oh, all right, Kennie, we'll go together, but surely there are some good things about the castle?'

'Maybe,' he conceded, 'but it's the horror that draws me all the time.'

'Well, I must say you've come to the right island.'

I set off with my bloodthirsty companion early one afternoon, running along the south side of the range which gave us a pretty spectacular view of the Mesaoria Plain below.

On these slopes below Buffavento is the Monastery of St Chrysostom and the Church of the Holy Trinity which has lately been restored. Kennie insisted on stopping.

'I've heard tell of the most marvellous old wooden door which belonged to the old church.'

'This one looks pretty old.'

'No, the original was pulled down and this *horror* put in its place.'

'Oh Kennie!'

But the door certainly was a magnificent piece of workmanship being made of many carved pieces put together without the use of nails. In the chapel there were also portions of the original floor which is set with coloured marbles.

The monastery is connected with the castle above for it is believed that the Queen of Buffavento, who lived here to be away from the violence of the Templars, suffered badly from leprosy and her small dog caught it from her. Each morning he disappeared down the mountain and after some days it was noticed that the dog was considerably better. The Queen had him followed and the servants found him bathing in a spring half way down the mountain. When she was told of this the Queen went herself to bathe and after a few days she also was cured. In gratitude she built the monastery and church for the Greek monks and placed it under the protection of St Chrysostom.

I can't say that our excursion up the mountain to Buffavento was a great success. We parked the Land-Rover under a huge olive tree and started up the rough track, falling and stopping all the time so that it took us about an hour to reach the top. But as we climbed the views became more and more beautiful and when, through a gap in the mountain we could see the much greener northern slopes and the beautiful coastline, Kennie was more than compensated.

'Even *I* am speechless,' he said breathlessly, 'worth all this torture' and I had difficulty in getting him to continue.

There was no custodian at the top for nothing remains but the walls that appear to grow out of the precipice sides. We clambered over parts of the summit and examined the sheer northern cliffs where the brother Montolif made his escape.

'See what I mean?' said Kennie, holding tightly on to my arm as he leaned over, 'the man couldn't have been human!'

'Anything rather than to be left up here, I should think.'

The castle's deterioration was hastened for the Venetians dismantled it, removing most of the roofs and armaments as they found it too difficult to garrison, and now it is little more than a crumbling mass of ruins.

'Well it's far too much of a ruin to have any ghosts,' I said, 'I told you it would be.'

Kennie shivered, 'I wouldn't spend a night up here,' he said, 'I just wouldn't.'

Already the wind had risen and it set up a curious whine. I wasn't sorry to follow my companion down the rocky track. 'Well,' he said when we finally climbed into the Land-Rover, 'I've had enough horror *and* fresh air for one day. Let's go to Clito's and chat up the Canadians.'

KANTARA – THE HAPPY ONE

You catch glimpses of Kantara Castle from many parts of the island; it stands like an old Viking ship, prodding the sky in a series of jagged pinnacles, at the end of the Kyrenia Range. Steep precipices fall away on three sides and from its ramparts the entire narrowing peninsula of Karpas tapers off below.

It is always satisfying returning to such places and Nancy and I picnicked here one fine day. It has a gayness the other castles lack and seems to revel in the careless disorder of its falling walls. A short walk takes you from the motor road to the main gate which is in a small enclosure with two towers. One of them has a turret with a series of small arches for defence and with a deep cistern cut in the rock below. On the opposite side a guardroom leads to a small narrow entrance where prisoners could pass through without the trouble of opening the main gates. Except for this area the castle is roofless and difficult to trace, but we wandered through the labyrinth of fallen stones and low walls that made quiet pockets for a picnic or to rest. As the ground rose to the west there was the roofless 'Queen's' chamber and a tiny chapel and here the stones appeared to have fallen quite recently.

There are few references to the castle's past history; perhaps because it was never used as a palace but as a watch tower and prison. There is mention of a long siege in 1225 by Royalist Forces but little else until the Venetians removed their garrison from here in 1525 and the place became deserted except for occasional people who sought sanctuary. There have been many tales of hidden treasure amongst the castle's foundations and probably the search for this has contributed to its bad state of repair. Just over fifty years ago it was necessary to strengthen the outer walls which were in danger of falling into the valley below.

We sat for a long time looking at the beautiful view from the tiny chapel and it was here that the castle's last inhabitant lived for many years. In 1876 Cesnola found an old Turkish hermit settled in the chapel; it had a roof in those days which gives some indication of the rapid rate of disintegration of the castle in comparison with the other ruins.

The hermit came from a village near Constantinople where, as a young man, he had a very beautiful wife and a good business, but an important and wealthy Turk living near by began taking an interest in the young wife and made proposals to her husband which he naturally rejected. Not long afterwards the husband was arrested on a completely unfounded charge and put in prison for three years. His house was burned down and his property destroyed, and his wife disappeared into the harem of the wealthy Turk.

Finally the young man was released on the condition that he leave Constantinople for ever. There was nothing he could do so he boarded a vessel that finally brought him to Cyprus, where, as Cesnola says: 'having lost his manhood, he roamed like a wild beast among the mountains living on herbs, olives and wild fruit...' At last he settled in the chapel, still living on wild olives and a little wheat he grew. The years went by and he became a complete hermit seeing no one except once a year, when followers of the Panayia Chapel climbed to the castle bringing tobacco, matches and a few provisions for the old man. By the time Cesnola arrived he had become so accustomed to his frugal way of life that all he asked of the Italian was a few matches. No one knows when he died or where he is buried, but one year the visitors must have arrived to find him no longer in need of their gifts.

As we moved out of the main gates I looked back. Perhaps the treasure still lies up there, buried deeper still by the rubble. Perhaps that is why the castle always seems to be smiling. . . .

13

Food – Beautiful Food!

My kitchen beneath the mulberry tree was too small for cooking complicated meals and my main diet at home had become salad, yoghurt, cheese, fruit – and beer. Brandy, at eight shillings a bottle was kept for guests, together with peanuts, although the cats ate most of these. Sometimes Nancy Verey came over in the evening for a drink and the menage came too, trailing in one after the other and settling on our laps or skylarking about. Even Bobbie John the oldest cat who was grumpy and resentful of the later 'upstarts' would finally arrive. They'd eat peanuts, yoghurt and cheese with great enthusiasm and were the most delightful and well-mannered family of animals I have ever met.

It wasn't necessary to lead such a frugal life, for in the café-cum-post office in the village, Georges always found something good for a meal, whilst Kyrenia was less than three miles away where there was the Harbour Club, Freddie's Restaurant – both on the harbour – an English 'Pub', Clito's Bar of *Bitter Lemons* fame, various other sometimes questionable clubs, and Theo's which was the best and cheapest place to eat.

With few exceptions the large hotels have indifferent international cooking, whereas both the Greek and Turkish food is delicious. Finding a place to eat is very simple for as well as those in the big towns and villages there are innumerable eating places along the coast. Cypriots and their families eat out all the time and I promised myself that some day I would arrange a gastronomic tour of the island, to include many of the Turkish restaurants as well.

Most of the restaurants and cafés have terraces and often in the early evening we would drive out to one or other of them; on a cliff top or in the shelter of a cove where, having ordered an ouzo or beer, the proprietor automatically brought a meze that could be anything from nuts and olives to a large array of hot and cold dishes. One's enthusiasm for these titbits often spurred him on to produce more and more.

Meals are ordered with as much serious concentration as you find with French families. There is a great use of herbs and spices and most dishes are cooked very slowly. Lamb, roasted with herbs and potatoes, is the most popular meat and a favourite dish with us all is Mousaka which is made of mince and vegetables including peppers, onions, courgettes, aubergine and tomatoes; sometimes white wine is added and the whole covered with a custard-like sauce and grated cheese. Another favourite is Dolmas which is stuffed vine leaves served with tomato or lemon sauce, and Sikotakia, which is chopped liver in wine with raw onions. Everyone cooks kebab fashion, portions of meat, kidney, bay leaves, bacon and mushrooms grilled on a skewer over a charcoal fire; but is there a country in the world that hasn't taken to this dish? Previously the larger brazier of coals with rows of skewers on top was a familiar sight in the streets, but now the custom is dying out.

People are beginning to buy the imported processed cheeses even though they have some very fine ones of their own. Fetta is the most popular and Kephalotiri which looks like Gruyère but has a very distinctive flavour. Yoghurt could be the national dish, for it can be found in the fridge of nearly every type of shop or café. The cartons are larger than our own and it is made by both the Greeks and the Turks.

Reluctantly one admits that Cypriot food is fattening but why not, for the locals like a little plumpness. I was often criticized for being too slim and advised to take just one egg-cup full of Commanderia each morning on waking. This, I was assured, would soon rectify my lack of curves. Many of the sweets are cooked with honey which gives them a delicious mellow flavour; and shamiski, a kind of pancake that is served with honey is delicious.

The wines, to be kind, are an acquired taste! They are too sweet, although dryer ones are gradually coming on the market. The red varieties are a little rough, but perhaps this counteracts the rich food as it does in Spain. One learns to drink them as one does the local beer, for all imported things are expensive and paying so much less for drinks makes social life easier and far more pleasant.

The islanders make good eating companions for they enjoy their food, whilst the British never *quite* throw caution to the wind. I was lunching with Kennie and we were sitting at midday in Theo's garden restaurant. Four tortoiseshell cats sat waiting expectantly, and around us were several couples from the British Sovereign Base. Kennie had just finished a large plate of foulia which is a very good dish of black beans, onions and tomatoes.

I was studying the menu. 'They've got shamiski,' I said.

'I never touch the sweets,' said Kennie, helping himself to a large orange, 'must think of the figure, you know. *Thank goodness* for all the fruit here. I just can't keep up, it comes along so quickly; soon there'll be apricots then peaches, nectarines, strawberries, figs and that *delicious* little thing that's a cross between a nectarine and a peach – trust the Cypriots to have invented that one.'

Theo brought our coffee himself. 'Your favourite cat has just had six kittens,' he said to me beaming, 'don't forget if you hear of anyone who would like to have one . . .'

'The *fertility* of it!' murmured my companion, as he helped himself to another orange.

A large snake was coiled up on the sunny garden path. It was so still it could have been dead and then it slithered into the undergrowth; which was as well, for our three *felis domestica* would most certainly have attacked it. This is an inborn instinct with all Cypriot cats and Nancy Verey tells of an earlier and much-loved one who fought with a snake in the field near by and then came home – to die.

All early travellers mention the cats of Cyprus and that the monasteries kept a great number for the sole purpose of attacking and killing snakes that were a great menace in the island. The Monastery of St Nicholas on the south coast had a great army of well-trained cats. Fr Suliano who visited the island in 1484 tells of the unceasing war waged between the cats and the snakes and how many of the cats had been badly maimed by the snakes and some had an eye or even two missing. He speaks about the strange sight of the cats returning from the fields at the sound of the midday bell, to have their food. Once having eaten, the bell tolled again and they left *en masse* for the fields, to continue their fight.

There are not so many snakes on the island today, but St Nicholas and other monasteries still keep a number of cats, and probably the Cypriots' refusal to kill them stems from those early days.

Most Cypriot cats are enchanting, they are very appreciative of everything and far better tempered than our own spoilt types. Perhaps they don't forget their luck in finding a good home and I have watched our three stand by towards the end of a meal, to allow some stray to finish the food. Many of them have the long thin tail of the original Egyptian and in recent years Siamese cats have been imported and some of their more outstanding characteristics can be recognized, even in the strays. Our own Biscuit, although a pale sandy colour – biscuit in fact – has the long thin body, small head and the gentle precious movements of the Siamese. In Lefka on the north coast, the cats are pink, but no one could tell me whether this is a unique breed or because of the red slag from the copper mines near by.

It is certain that cat lovers and especially the British, are well advised *not* to settle in Cyprus for the cats have an unerring instinct in locating such people. Many European families have twelve or more and kittens are always being left on the doorstep. The refusal to kill has something of the Buddhist 'cruelty' where one sees diseased animals lying around temples, often in great pain and slowly starving to death. Here in Cyprus kittens are left on the roads where there are three alternatives; they may be picked up by some kind-hearted person, or be maimed and crawl away to die; or they are killed outright by a vehicle – but of course not by their original owner.

Dogs are definitely in the minority and most of them are the descendants of the well-bred hunting dogs brought in by the British in the last century. It is the small animals and insects that are the most unpleasant in Cyprus and one night a large hairy tarantula chased me round the bedroom floor. There were never many wild and ferocious animals here although in the mountains asses and stags were found, but even the leopard was tamed to hunt these other animals. The island's *moufflon* was threatened with extinction until the authorities put a preservation order on them, and now once again their numbers are increasing. They are timid and difficult to see except in the reserve station at Stavros tis Psokas in the Paphos Forest. They resemble the *moufflon* found on the fringes of the Sahara.

Many of our neighbours kept donkeys and we saw them in most of the villages, but the camel is becoming quite rare and works mainly on the Mesoaria Plain. There are foxes and hares in the hills, but it is the birds, not the animals, that bring the island to life, for as well as the inhabitants, it is a great *caravanserai* for their migrations and more than three hundred species have been seen in the island. From the higher parts of the mountains we caught glimpses of vultures and buzzards, and once an eagle made his disturbing flight overhead. There are some Little Owl and Scops Owl and along the slopes of the range there are many rock doves and the Cyprus Warbler which is found nowhere else but on the island.

The francolin is difficult to locate for it has been badly overshot and is seldom seen anywhere but in the Karpas. Now the birds are being protected and the old custom of trapping them with tree-lime spread on bushes, is controlled by permits which are given at certain times.

In the winter the salt lake near Larnaca is a beautiful sight and a paradise for bird lovers. Flocks of flamingoes settle and the grey haze turns to flame red as they move; later there are egrets, herons and ibises as well. With the regularity that would be the envy of any railway commuter, mass migrations of cranes and storks fly over the island, stopping one night on their way to Egypt. Many times in England I have watched the swallows assembling with all the chatter and bustle of a proposed expedition. It was fine now to see them arrive *en route* – as they do with unfailing regularity in the middle of February – like meeting up with friends last seen before a journey began.

14

The Men of the Forests

Nancy's hotel was modern and near the waterfront in Kyrenia. Many of the U.N. officers came here for a short leave and their off duty behaviour was not always exemplary. And who could wonder? Feminine society of the better kind is very scarce, for no respectable Cypriot girl is allowed out on a blind date and without parental supervision. In the summer, tourists bring some light-hearted diversion; but now it was spring. It was no wonder that in their boredom they frequented the clubs and bars more than was wise, and this state of affairs culminated in a scandal when some young Canadians beat up the much-respected Clito in his bar. After the reprimands and the inquiry things became a little quieter. Nancy, no doubt, received the full force of their adulation but she, with the singleness of purpose that I admired so much was, 'getting on with her writing'; swimming for exercise; and coming occasionally to the Little Hut to drink home-brewed tea. The social life of Kyrenia was not for me and I left from time to time on jaunts that could take anything from a day to a week. At the moment my attention was on the forests which have a special fascination no matter where they are; and the men who work in them have a quality all their own. The conservation of the forests is important to the island and the State Forestry Reserves that were started by the British are being carried on and enlarged all the time. There are several reserves in the island with the main ones in the Troodos and Paphos Mountains and along the Kyrenia Range. I visited these with Sir Harry Luke who was making one of his many visits to the island as he had been doing for over half a century. He came as Private Secretary to the High Commissioner of Cyprus in 1911 and returned later as Commissioner of Famagusta. I have read his books and heard tales of him as a raconteur and a charming person, in places as far apart as Malta and Fiji where he was Governor in the years 1938 to 1942. It was almost impossible to believe that such a quick inquiring mind could belong to someone of his age. He loved Cyprus and there was little he didn't know about it. We had quiet meals along the coast in little fishing cafés or explored a monastery or church; but mainly we penetrated the forests of the Kyrenia Range which, with the Karpas, were Sir Harry's favourite parts of the island.

The Kyrenia Forests have a gentle air that is almost Italian in character and as we drove along the thickly wooded Khalevga area there were glimpses of the Mesaoria Plain to the south and breathtaking vistas of the northern slopes which never cease to give a shock of pleasure. We visited the Forest Station headquarters and there was a great stillness under the blanket of branches. Later we dipped down along the northern slopes to the Monastery of Antiphonitis which is protected by a small narrow valley. It is uninhabited now except for an occasional custodian monk, but the small twelfth-century church is in good repair and so is the set of cells near by. There was no one around but the glimpses of the church's tiled dome and roof, nestling in the curve of the valley as we bumped down the rough winding track, was especially exciting.

For some years after Sir Harry first came to the island these places could not be reached except by mule, horse or on foot and he spoke of the island as quite enchanted in those times. After World War II the British Administration started to construct forest roads both here and in the Troodos Mountains and the Cypriots have continued to build more.

'Go and see the Troodos Mountains,' Sir Harry said, 'they are very grand, but these hills hold an enchantment for me' . . . he looked along the waves of mauve hills and smiled. His next visit was to be his final one for he died on the island.

I set out one morning for Nicosia and the Forest Department Headquarters. One of the nicest things about Cypriots is their accessibility and even those at the top will see you if you persevere. I had an appointment with Mr Seraphim the acting Director.

It wasn't necessary for me to wait for the U.N. convoy that leaves Kyrenia each morning and shepherds all the Greek-Cypriot cars through the Turkish enclave, for by now I was well known at the Turkish check point and in the villages I passed through. Now that the tension had eased I wondered if the border checks and convoys were really necessary, although another incident could trigger off more fighting and nobody felt absolutely secure. Right at the beginning when I had driven alone into the enclave, Turkish officials and the civilians alike seemed touched by my refusal to admit that anything was amiss; I have seen the same look on faces when driving into an oasis in the desert hundreds of miles from any European. I often stopped in the Turkish villages and bought fruit or yoghurt and it was a great day when restrictions were taken off petrol and I could fill up my tank at a Turkish station.

Mr Seraphim was a handsome young man who had taken a course in England. 'Yes,' he said, 'you can go and see the work in the forests. I shall let them know you are coming.' It was as simple as that.

You can approach the Troodos Mountains from all sides and I took the north-west road, as it passes near Peristerona which has the beautiful medieval church of the Saints Barnabas and Hilarion. It stands near a small river and is large, with five domes that form a perfect silhouette. I never cease to be entranced by the outlines of these churches against the blue sky; and by the warm glow of the sun on the stones that gives them a *living* quality.

I climbed out of the Land-Rover and finally went inside – although it was the silhouette and the gold and blue that I had come to see. Nancy would have called me a Philistine! The church has some finely carved old doors but the narthex is a later addition. The iconostasis is sixteenth century with an icon of the Presentation of the Temple of the same period, and a kneeling donor dressed in red with a black cloak. The portraits of the donars in the churches give a vivid and human picture of the people of the day and make it easier to identify the period.

As I turned south the road began to climb into the mountains and the valleys were deeper and darker and very different from our own soft Kyrenia Range with its pinnacles of castles and the gentle rich Italian colours. Already there were wooden chalets clinging to the sides of the valley reminiscent of Switzerland.

Previously the whole area was heavily conscious of the British who used the mountains as a holiday resort and rest camp and there had been the insularity of an Indian Hill Station. It is still a favourite place for holidays as it has always been, for even the Venetians visited the mountain monasteries to get away from the humid summer months in the plains below.

I was driving along the base of the Solean Valley which became narrower as the road climbed into the mountains. Some of the finest frescoes in the island are found in the churches in these valleys and I passed through Galata which has several of them. A mile farther on I came to Kakopetria which straggles along both sides of the stream as it narrows into a gorge. Suddenly the road opens out into a wide square of restaurants, hotels and giant poplars which form a cool umbrella over the whole centre. The town is little more than an hour's fast run in from the capital and is already 2,200 feet above the sea and its shady terraces attract many day visitors as well as the holiday makers.

I inquired about the Church of St Nicholas of the Roof which lies roughly three miles off the main road. A small boy offered to come with me and show the way; he was slight with large soft brown eyes, and was determined to practise his English on me. We climbed into very wooded country and came to a plateau where the church stands. The exterior masonry and workmanship is crude in comparison with most local churches and it belonged to a monastery that ceased to exist in the last century. The church was built in the eleventh century and certain additions were added later. But the most unusual feature is the steep pitched outer roof of flat tiles that was added later to protect the building from the snow. The interior is very beautiful and is entirely covered with frescoes painted from the eleventh to the thirteenth centuries and with many portraits of donors. It was difficult however to see some of the frescoes for the antiquities department had erected scaffolding and were cleaning and repairing them. A large fourteenth-century icon of St Nicholas is painted on vellum and kept in a glass case. Most of the frescoes are in very good condition, due probably to the added protection of the outer roof. Many fine frescoes have already been ruined in some of the churches because of the damp and want of repairs to roofs.

Near the church were signs of a recently dismantled military camp, the ground was laid out with whitewashed stones and in the centre was an inscription.

'What does it say, Nicos?'

He struggled with the translation: 'Enclose in your soul (or heart) Greece and then you will feel every sign of greatness.'

When we returned to Kakopetria I gave Nicos some money, 'To buy a book you might want,' I said.

He took it and smiled. 'I would be glad to come with you – to Troodos,' he said, 'the Land-Rover and you – is very splendid.'

But I went off alone and the road became steep as it took wide turns and opened out finally to show a bare mountain of huge slag heaps which came from the Amiandos Asbestos Mines and the sterile grey dust fell away to the valley below. The mines, which have been working for over sixty years, are amongst the largest in the world. Minerals have been found in the mountains since ancient times and many strange tales were told of this particular substance which they called Amianthus. It was found in stone and spun into thread from which they made cloth that was incombustible and could be cleaned by fire. Shrouds were made of it and so the ashes from the burnt bodies were kept separate from the fuel.

Mr. Jacovides was the officer in charge of the Troodos Forest Division headquarters at Plantania and we studied the map of the State Forests which also marks the many areas where goats are prohibited. Having seen lands turned into deserts by these beasts, the law seems a brilliant one. We drove to the tree nursery where varieties of pines, acacia and silver fir were set out in rows. Trees are in demand for new areas that are to be re-afforested and also to replace those destroyed by fire. Experiments were proving successful in finding a tree that would grow on the Amiandos slag heaps. Along the roads, cut into the mountainside, *acacia phendassasia* has been planted to arrest erosion and the light green leaves give a nice contrast to the darker pines.

Every Cypriot understands the need for trees and each year there is a tree planting ceremony which was started by the British and carried on by both Greek and Turkish Cypriots.

The Turkish community have their ceremonies on the 18th and 25th December and the Greeks in January.

'Do you lose a lot of trees through fire?' I asked. 'I thought Cypriots were very conscious of the risk.'

'Sometimes they start carelessly or with a piece of glass on bracken, but the worst ones are those started maliciously, during an emergency. That is why we build more and more roads so that it is easier to reach the fires.'

We were making our way towards the highest point in the island, the breast-shaped Olympus and from the summit there is an uninterrupted view of most of the island. On the site was a temple dedicated to Aphrodite Acraea that was forbidden to women, nor could they look at it. According to Aristotle many plants that were used in healing grew on the mountain. The Venetians built a small fort here but made no effort to defend it against the Turks and surrendered immediately. Nothing remains of the fort and during the Turkish occupation the place was completely deserted except for the peasants who came up to gather snow to be sold in the capital.

'Now,' said my companion as we pulled up, 'you will meet Allah. He has been firewatcher and caretaker here for seventeen years.'

'Allah?' Could he possibly be a Turk?

'We call him Allah because he is above everyone else.'

Such is the impartiality of the Forest Men.

A cheery little man in a woolly cap came towards us. 'I'm just making a cup of tea. Will you have some?' he said.

'Thanks.' The whole of the island lay below us and we found our bearings by direction dial.

Allah put two mugs on the table, and came over to us. 'I've looked at that for seventeen years and never get tired of it,' he said. 'This is where Noah landed with his ark, you know,' and he gave me a knowing nod as he went back into the hut.

There is a Met. station and the radio transmitter for the island, but it would be a lonely place when tensions run high. Allah, with the same sense of fatalism as his namesake, was quite unperturbed.

'Think,' he said as he poured out the tea, 'what folk would pay for such a view and I have it – free.'

The winter season had finished but the hotel at the Troodos resort remains open. There are a couple of shops, a Forest Station and some houses set on the flat plateau which is carefully laid out for the winter periods. We passed the camp for the British personnel from the Sovereign Base Area and inspected some new plantings of *pinus brudia* and cedar on a bleak headland.

I inquired about the summer residence of the British Governors.

'It is seldom used now,' said my companion, 'occasionally Archbishop Makarios spends the night there. Would you like to see it?'

'Yes, if there is no one in residence.'

We drove along a narrow track which was heavily shrouded by tall pines and came to a buff where the trees were larger and closer together. We stopped at a wooden gate beside a row of huts. Beyond in the trees stood a curious Victorian building surrounded by lawns that ran to the edge of the buff. The grey house was closed and shuttered, a tasteless relic in beautiful surroundings.

More than once during my travels I have crossed the path of the French vagabond poet and rebel against society, Arthur Rimbaud. The last time was in Harar, Ethiopia where a long two-storey wooden house is pointed out as being the one in which he lived.

When the British arrived in Cyprus in 1878 a camp was set up for the troops in Troodos and three years later it was decided to build a summer residence for the Governor here. The supervision of it was given to Rimbaud. What strange course of events brought him here? He had already deserted from the Dutch army and lived in the forests of Java before coming to Cyprus where he took a job at £6 a month as overseer at a stone quarry. Not long afterwards he became ill and returned to France but was back again in 1881 and took on the task of building the residence at £8 a month. From his letters it would seem he was disenchanted with life at this time and says nothing of the beauty of the island, complaining endlessly of the heat, the various diseases, and pleading for text books on architecture and surveying. He left the island with no regrets and departed for Harar. He died in Marseilles at the age of thirty-seven having known every hardship and poverty in Paris, joined and deserted from the French army, made money and spent it in Africa, trading in everything from ivory and guns to slaves, escaped attempted murder by his friend Verlaine and intrigued with Menelik the Lion of Judah to build his Empire. His life with its restless wanderings leave so many queries that cannot be answered and make him one of the most enigmatic characters of the last century.

Even this ugly building we were looking at is a contradiction and gives no clue to the man, as it stands shuttered and hemmed in by the dark pines.

It was cold and clear when I set off to the west next morning for the Paphos Forest which is very different in character, for the forests face the sun and the southern slopes have vines and orchards. I spent the previous night at the hotel in Troodos. In the bar-cum-general store attached to the hotel the local lads had foregathered. We had ouzo, beer or brandy and talked of the skiing season just finished and toasted Icarius as the first man to make wine. Cypriots are full of surprises for they have varied and mixed pieces of knowledge. One day I went swimming with a young artist who quoted extensively from the works of Alice Baker.

An excellent road runs from Troodos to the north coast and after ten miles I turned off it to the left. I slowed up, adjusting myself to the different tempo as the road wound round the slopes past Kykko Monastery which looked deserted and shut in on itself. From here the left road skirts Mount Tripylos and runs through the beautiful cedar forest. The trees (*brevifolia*) are indigenous to the island and were threatened with extinction until a protection order was put on them. The air was warmer and two turtle doves rose from the road as I drove up.

Finally the road took me to the end of the Stavros Valley and Stavros tis Psokas, the headquarters of the Paphos Forest District. The settlement is sheltered by the hills which are densely wooded. On one side was a cluster of houses for the workers and opposite were the offices, a small café and a Rest House. Mr Lambrianides, the officer in charge had been through it all, the British period, the EOKA troubles, independence, and now the Turkish-Greek emergencies. He had seen the forest set alight during the British time and again in 1964 and it could happen again any day.

I recognized the Rest House from my previous visit when my presence had been frowned upon as I was not 'official'. Now a couple of families lived here and there was a constant flow of people coming and going. The building was an oblong, wooden structure set against the steep slopes and a little apart, with wide verandas on both floors. The furniture – uniform government issue – was the same, and some of the exclusiveness, the sense of superiority of the British lingered in the austere rooms.

The enclosure for the *moufflon* was near by. The animals ran for cover and looked depressed and dull of coat. Even the bare rocks and wadis of the desert would have been preferable to this dreary confined space.

I spent two days in the Rest House and the men took me with them when they made the rounds of the forest huts. In the valleys we were permanently in the shadow of the trees, and we delved deeper still looking for the men who were felling and were guided by the sound of the saws. We followed the valley of the Livadhi which runs out to the sea near the fishing village of Pomos. One of the foresters pointed to the bare hill which spread across the horizon between us and the sea.

'That was once a forest,' he said.

'And what's beyond?'

'Oh, that's the Turkish enclave of Kokkina,' he said, 'during the fighting in 1964 they dropped bombs – the Turks – just east of the enclave over there,' pointing to our right, 'there was fighting and the fires went on for a week.'

We continued along the valley towards the sea. It was a sheltered little valley with a small stream and as it took a deep turn we came to a small hamlet that was burnt out and abandoned.

'It was a Turkish settlement,' he said, 'I hope that some time they will be able to come back.'

Perhaps I had seen these people who fled in the night to Kokkina. It was a beautiful little place to remember. We drove on towards the sea and I wondered how any outsider could live on the island and not be torn to pieces by these divided loyalties.

There is an element of being dropped into another land about the Sovereign Base with its ordered lay-out and air of quiet efficiency. But the island seems to accept and adjust to the Base personnel just as it has done in earlier times with the Armenians and the Moronites. I returned by the south coast road to spend the weekend at the British Sovereign Base with the Army Commander-in-Chief Major-General Lloyd Owen and his wife. My old Land-Rover looked a little incongruous as it was driven away from the elegant covered porch.

Flagstaff House stands in the western point of Episkopi and is a fine but not too large house with a wide lounge opening on to a comfortably furnished terrace veranda, making the garden and terrace one. On the edge of the rose bed was a private helicopter landing-ground with the cliffs and sea beyond.

A young major who had just returned from the Libyan desert lunched with us. The expedition had been sponsored by the General himself and his own exploits in that part of the world during the last war make him a legend in his own time. Our talk was naturally about the desert for it was the link that brought us together, as it has always done for travellers over the centuries.

15

The Last of the Lusignans

The female who travels in remote places meets far more men than women which is rather unsatisfactory and unbalanced. Entire feminine company is even worse and during a crisis, or because of an accident, I have been thrust into a harem and smothered with femininity. After such an experience it is a relief to return to the more ordinary state of affairs.

Cyprus is certainly not remote and the women are very much in evidence, but in general they are happy with their families and homes, and the casual acquaintance isn't of great interest to them. I had been fortunate in meeting Nancy but now she had returned to England. I missed her company and our trips together.

Women have not played a prominent part in the island's history despite the cult of Aphrodite but there are a few who made colourful if brief appearances. There was the energetic St Helena who brought religious relics and stayed just long enough to build churches in an attempt to convert the heathen; and the beautiful Empress Theodora whose Cypriot father Akakios was the bear keeper of the Hippodrome in Constantinople. Would she have risen to such dizzy heights if as a child she had stayed on the island? Most certainly her fragile beauty would not have been perpetuated as it is today in the mosaic of the Church of San Vitale in Ravenna. No appearance was quite so brief as that of Umm Harum who had scarcely set foot on the island before the fatal fall from her mule. Even so she still receives homage from Muslim ships as they pass within sight along the coast.

Catherine Cornaro has a far more definite place in the island's history, although it is not in Cyprus but in the larger galleries all over Europe that one sees portraits of this Venetian girl who became the last Queen of Cyprus. They show her as comely and well proportioned in the fashion of the fifteenth century, although except for one obscure artist's work and two portraits by Bellini, it is doubtful if many are authentic. Even the Titian in the Uffizi in Florence, which portrays her as a young girl, could not have been taken from life, for Titian was too young at the time. Nevertheless she captured the imagination of the artists and poets of the day, when as a child of fifteen, James II of Cyprus asked for her hand in marriage and the Republic of Venice subsequently adopted her as a daughter to further its own political and territorial ambitions.

There had been little drama in Catherine's life until then and there were few diversions for the daughter of a nobleman in the fifteenth century in Venice. Hours of her time were spent on the terrace roof of her father's palace; on her head was a broad-brimmed crownless hat and over the brim her hair spread out, each strand carefully separated so that the strong sunlight could bleach it a rich Venetian gold, which was the colour all the beauties of the day aspired to.

At this time the Venetian nobleman's views of domestic matters were influenced by Byzantium and his women were as jealously guarded as those in an eastern Seraglio. Their wives seldom left the house and it was the courtesans who were seen on the piazza, dressed in brilliant colours, or passing in their gondolas along the canals. Their doings and sayings were of great interest and it was to their salons he went, not his own home, if he wanted to meet the poets, artists and musicians of the day. His wife appeared only on grand occasions, festivals and at the Ducal Palace when he took great care to see that at such times his mistress did not outshine his wife, at least in her dress. When he was away from home he made certain that some trusted servant guarded his womenfolk, and it was no wonder that he encouraged the barbarous fashion then in vogue of wearing plattens, for these high iron shoes of enormous size made it almost impossible for a woman to move around without the support of at least two people, one on each side.

The life of a nobleman's daughter was even less exciting for she never attended the banquets and her clothes were even more simple. She had no jewellery except perhaps a small gold cross on a chain and she seldom left the house except for short visits to a girl friend when she was carefully chaperoned by an old nurse. Her one wish was that a marriage should be arranged when at least she could choose her own clothes; and have the opportunity of acquiring ropes and ropes of large pearls which was the one ambition of all Venetian ladies. Such was Catherine Cornaro's life until James sent his ambassador Poplocataro to ask for her hand in marriage.

James's background and life were very different. He was the son of John II of Cyprus and his beautiful mistress Marietta from whom he inherited immense charm, good looks and a flamboyant personality. His mother lost her good looks later when John II's wife Queen Helena, in a fit of jealous rage, bit off the tip of her nose. James was a great favourite with everyone and after his father's death he had little opposition when he returned to the island and seized the throne – quite illegally – from his half sister Charlotte who had been made Queen. After fleeing to Kyrenia Castle with her husband, where she lived in a state of siege for nearly four years, Charlotte finally retired to Rome. And for the next twenty years she made repeated efforts to return as queen to Cyprus but without success.

No sooner was James established on the throne than the Signory of Venice turned its attention to the young usurper. They realized the importance of an alliance which would be consolidated if a Venetian bride could be found for the king. Also, the Turks were becoming too strong in the area and it was imperative to keep Cyprus from falling into their hands.

Amongst James's friends was the wealthy nobleman from Venice, Andrea Cornaro, who was Catherine's uncle. He pointed out to the king the advantages of having the Republic of Venice as his best ally and it has been said that Cornaro dropped a miniature of his niece on the floor and the king picked it up. The portrait was beautiful and from that moment he became interested.

When James finally sent his ambassador to Venice to ask for Catherine's hand, the Senate accepted, promising also to adopt her as a daughter of the Republic so that she would not be inferior in any way to her husband. To this was added the handsome dowry of one hundred thousand ducats.

In 1468 the ceremony of betrothal took place by proxy in Venice and was celebrated in great splendour at the Ducal Palace. Forty ladies of noble birth brought Catherine from the

Palazzo Cornaro to the palace where she was received by the Doge Christforo Moro, the Council state officials and the senators. James's proxy Filippo Mastachelli placed the consecrated ring on her finger and she was formally given away to James Lusignan by the Doge. Then with great ceremony she was escorted by her Court to her palace at Sal Polo.

Four years passed, however, before Catherine sailed for Cyprus. In the meantime she was treated as a queen by the Venetians, although after a while there were doubts that she would eventually become one, for Ferdinand of Naples was secretly trying to break up the alliance in favour of a match with one of his own daughters. Venice was determined to hold James to his pledges and an ambassador was sent to Cyprus to reason with the king. It was pointed out that the whole issue would be made public and everyone would know that James had gone back on his word; to say nothing of the insult to Catherine herself. Finally Venice promised to take the island under its protection the moment the king carried out the agreement. The strong stand and the promises influenced James and he agreed to go ahead. There is no doubt also that the king's preference had been towards Catherine all along.

Now preparations were made for Catherine's departure. On 14th July 1472 she was brought to the Church of St Mark. Before the high Altar the Doge made her a Child of the Republic, and she became Catherine Veneta Lusignan, a daughter of Venice. The city celebrated the occasion in a grand manner with colourful and splendid festivities and two months later the ship *Bucentaur* arrived to take her to the island. In a gold gown and with a long train, she moved down the steps of her palace, towards the Doge who gave her his hand. They sat side by side on the dais as the ceremonial barge slid slowly down the Grand Canal and out to the Lido where the *Bucentaur*, surrounded by a fleet of smaller ships, waited to take her to Cyprus.

16

Catherine Cornaro

'Give me the world if Thou wilt, but grant me an asylum for my affections.' TULKA

Catherine was eighteen, beautiful by all accounts and her marriage to the attractive James was a happy one. However less than a year after her arrival her husband, out shooting near Famagusta, was suddenly taken ill with pains from which he never recovered. He was only thirty-three and there were accusations from the enemies of Venice that his death was due to poison; but the low-lying parts of the island were notoriously unhealthy and many people died from fever and malaria.

Catherine, left a widow, was already pregnant and in his will James had bequeathed his kingdom to his queen and the child. He also left two illegitimate sons, Eugenio and Giovanni and a daughter named Zarla and he had decreed that the crown should revert first to the sons and then to Zarla in the event of Catherine and her child's death. Now there was no chance of Charlotte, the rightful heir regaining the throne.

Catherine's son James was born seven weeks after his father's death and troubles for the Queen had already begun. The Cypriot nobles were jealous of Venetian power and the Archbishop of Nicosia persuaded them to encourage Ferdinand of Naples as a counterbalance to the strength of Venice. (As well as this Charlotte made another bid to regain the throne.) Whilst Catherine was still recovering from the birth of her son in the palace of Famagusta, and the Venetian fleet had already left, the Archbishop together with the Counts of Jaffa and Tripoli, and Marin Rizzo who had all been named by James to form a council, rose in revolt. Their idea was to marry Alfonzo the son of Ferdinand of Naples to James's daughter Zarla and claim the throne in this way. As a first step they seized the city of Famagusta, forcing their way into the palace and into Catherine's own apartment where her physician

Gabriel Gentile had fled for safety. He was killed by Marin in front of the Queen. Both her uncle Andrea and her cousin Marco Bembo were stabbed and their bodies left in the moat beneath the Queen's windows, where they stayed for many days. The baby was taken from his mother and Alfonzo was proclaimed Prince of Galilee. Catherine was forced to write to the Venetian Senate explaining that the deaths of her uncle and cousin were due to a quarrel between them and the soldiers, over pay. But the correct report of the whole affair was sent by the Venetian consul, and Mocenigo, the Admiral of the Venetian fleet was ordered to sail again for Cyprus. When he arrived he found the people in Famagusta and Nicosia had risen in support of their Queen and were demanding her release. As well as this the conspirators were quarrelling amongst themselves and fled in disorder. Some of them were caught and executed, and gradually order was restored.

For further safety the towns and forts were put in the hands of those who were known to be loyal to the Republic. Venice had, by her prompt action and protection of the Queen, established a right to participate in the running of the island and now slowly but firmly she began to take control. The next year a *provveditore* and two counsellors were sent from Venice to assist Catherine.

Unfortunately a few days before his first birthday Catherine's son died. Her father was sent to comfort his daughter and also to be on hand to assist the counsellors should there be any revolt following the young prince's death.

Now without an heir Catherine's position was not a happy one. Whether she kept her throne or not depended on Venice. Her movements were restricted and most of her time was spent in Famagusta and Nicosia, the cities faithful to her. Her income which was controlled by the counsellors was cut to a minimum and above all, she could never contemplate marrying again for then the control of the island would go from the Republic. Her life depended on the strength of the Venetian garrison for there were constant intrigues by some of the Cypriot nobles and they naturally counted their own peasants with them. They realized the Queen had no real power and conspiracies were constantly being discovered with threats of revolution, dethronement and danger to Catherine's life. Naturally this situation was also far from satisfactory to Venice.

For ten years Catherine ruled in this way, having less and less liberty and being treated almost with suspicion. In spite of her position or perhaps because of it, many of her subjects had grown fond of her and were extremely loyal. They resented the taut atmosphere between her and Venice and the severe treatment she had to endure; also they feared the intention of the Republic to take over the island completely.

The whole situation came to a head in 1488 when Venice was forced by two eventualities to make a stand. It had become clear that the Sultan Bajazet II, who intended to subdue the mamelukes of Egypt, would try to take Cyprus as a base, and at the same time Alfonzo of Naples had decided to ask for Catherine's hand. This threw Venice into a panic, for a second marriage was far more dangerous than any plot to overthrow the Queen, and it was finally decided that Catherine must be recalled.

After a meeting of the Council of Ten, Pruili, the Admiral of the fleet was ordered to carry out the mission and Catherine's brother Giorgio Cornaro was sent with him to help persuade his sister. They were instructed to tell her that should she refuse to abdicate she would cease to be under the protection of the Republic, her income would stop and she would be treated as a rebel.

When the two men arrived they were met with indignant opposition. Catherine was angry, she wept and she pleaded, 'Is it not enough,' she asked, 'that Venice shall inherit when I am gone?' But the men had their orders and nothing but a complete abdication would do. They promised that she would continue to be treated as royalty and that she was to receive a large income on her retirement. Finally she was forced to give way.

The Republic intended to leave no doubt that the Queen was abdicating of her own free will and insisted on public ceremonies of abdication. The first took place in her favourite city, Famagusta on February 26th 1489, where in the main square solemn *Te Deums* were sung. The Queen watched from beneath a *baldachino* as the flag of the Lusignan was lowered and the banner of St Mark took its place. Then she left the city no longer a Queen.

The ceremony was repeated in Nicosia and every town and village that had been her own. The islanders gathered round her, increasing in numbers and they wept at her departure – and for their lost liberty. Finally, when the whole farce was over, Catherine and her brother sailed for Venice.

Her reception on returning to Venice was as spectacular as her departure had been; and for three days there were banquets and festivities with one final ceremony before the Republic would let her go. At St Mark, where eighteen years earlier she became the Daughter of Venice, Catherine made her last act of abdication.

The Republic gave Catherine the little lordship of Asolo which lies north of Venice. The village and castle rise above vineyards and orchards and there is a magnificent backcloth of the Dolomites beyond. Here, with her Court of twelve maids of honour and eighty serving men, her hounds, apes, peacocks and a favourite Negress to look after the parrots, she became a patron of the arts and scholars of the Renaissance. Life was very peaceful. She divided her time between the castle and a country house she built on the plain below which is used today by Trevisan farmers and is known as the Barco della Regina Cornaro. Peitro Bembo composed his Asolini around her Court and he invented the verb *asolare* which means 'to disport in the open air – to amuse oneself at random'.

This pleasant existence continued for ten years when the penetration of the Imperial troops into Trevisano made it necessary for her to return to her father's palace in Venice, where she died a year later. Catherine was buried with as much splendour as the fast depleting coffers of the Republic could afford.

I searched in vain for clues, relics or even ghosts of Catherine in Cyprus but there is little to find; not much more than the graves in Famagusta of her Lusignan husband and their small son. But in Asolo she still dominates the scene. True, it is now a tourist town and Catherine's castle has been turned into a cinema with a terrace café of bright tables and sunshades; but in the church is the fine altarpiece by the young Lorenzo Lotto that Catherine commissioned; and a new baptistry has been built to house the font which lay for so long out of sight and forgotten. It bears the insignia of the Lusignan Kingdoms of Cyprus and Armenia; and a stone panel with her arms in the small museum near by must be the last engraving to bear the emblem. As you come out, the great iron bell rings from the castle's tower; and the mellow tones can be heard far down through the vineyards, towards the plain. . . .

17

Hard Heritage

'Somehow good will be the final goal of ill.'

Even today Greek Cypriots still speak with surprise of the unexpected and instantaneous flare-up of Ethniki Organosis Kypriou Agoniston (EOKA), for secretly EOKA had collected followers who infiltrated to the remotest of villages. One day the ordinary folk were going about their business and the next no one trusted his neighbour. Old scores were settled in the name of EOKA and anyone known to have worked or lived peacefully beside the British was uneasy and often a marked man. Fear must certainly have been the motive that turned the pleasure-loving Greek Cypriot into a violent killer; fear not so much of the British but of the organization and wave of hate that held them. The main target, naturally, was the British and any underground fighting organization is not gentle or ethical in its killing. Innocent civilians were killed for no other reason than they were British; the customs official and his pregnant wife who were ambushed at the crossroad on the Kyrenia Range where I had stopped, hand grenades were thrown into the car killing the wife immediately and the wounded husband, trying to reverse the car, was set upon, badly beaten and finally killed with a shot gun. A British doctor attending a patient – brought in by the man who now killed him; and the army chaplain, his wife and child who had a grenade thrown into their house as they sat at lunch. Even the schoolgirls participated when a group of them organized a procession through the narrow streets of Nicosia, to lure the British security guards who were following to protect them, right into their brothers' fire.

In February 1956 the Abbot of Chrysorrhoyiatissa Monastery was sitting with some of his brothers listening to the radio when two men dressed as monks broke into the room and shot him at close range. He died immediately. The Abbot had been friendly with the British and was killed because of a false report that he had betrayed two EOKA members. Archbishop Makarios officiated at the Abbot's funeral, blessing both the EOKA men and the 'traitor'!

And the killing did not end with victory and independence. A man from a village on the Kyrenia Range who had continued to work for the British as a handyman, finally returned to see his wife at his village. EOKA members sought him out and in front of his wife poured petrol over him, set it alight and he was burnt to death. The former Minister of the Interior Polykarpas Yeorkadjis shot his way out of hospital and his exploits are still talked about. Today in many churches there are portraits and photographs of local heroes who either killed some Britisher or were killed themselves.

But many Cypriots who were educated in England felt certain loyalties that were difficult to relinquish and they were best away from the island. Now those troubles lie in the past, but the island has others of its own for once again there are the two communities that fight and are moving more and more apart. Must this always happen? And what strange motivation, driving force, has brought this unhappy, unnecessary state of affairs into being?

I sat in the hall of the Presidential Palace and felt dwarfed by the high walls. There was no sound whatsoever. Opposite were large double doors and occasionally someone approached them to give a discreet knock and then enter. When they returned there was that look on people's faces when they have just left the presence of someone unassailably their superior in some way.

Peter came towards me down the long hall. His feet made no noise on the soft carpeted floor.

'He'll see you alone,' he said, with a slight nuance of surprise.

'No interpreter?' I was glad, for they are inhibiting to a novice like myself and are often used merely to give the person time to study the questions.

'No interpreter,' Peter confirmed, 'he understands a lot, but speak slowly.' I nodded. 'But then you often speak with other nationalities,' and he smiled his warm Cypriot smile that was endearing at this moment for I was about to meet His Beautitude Archbishop Makarios, President of the Republic of Cyprus.

Peter returned down the long hall and there was still no noise, no bustle – a calm setting for a man with so much on his plate. All this grandeur was familiar to him now, for it is ten years since he took up duties as President of the Republic. Beyond the large windows many limousines were parked on the circular drive and well-kept lawns spread over the high flat ground. My mind flashed back to Ano Panayia the small village in the Paphos Hills where, as Michael Christodoulou Mouskos, the President was born a year before the First World War. At what age was it apparent that this farmer's son would strive for other, bigger things? He attended the village school until at thirteen he became a novice at Kykko Monastery. He went from here to the Pancyprian Gymnasium in Nicosia, the best school in the island. Later he was awarded the Kykko scholarship to the School of Theology of Athens University and he remained in Greece during the German occupation. As well as his ordinary work he studied Law for two years and when he was ordained in 1946 he took the name of Makarios which means 'Blessed'. He interrupted his legal studies to take up another scholarship awarded to him by the World Council of Churches for post graduate studies at the University of Boston in the U.S.A. And so his horizon was broadening all the time. He was still in Boston in 1948 when word came that he had been elected Bishop of Kitium; and he likes to relate that this was not the first time the church had approached him to return to Cyprus and that previously he had refused. When he returned and was enthroned as Bishop, Makarios embarked on a campaign for the island's liberation which was to last in some form or another until independence. During the following year he visited King Paul and the Greek Prime Minister to discuss the handling of the Cyprus question. When the Archiepiscopal throne became vacant he was unanimously elected as the island's Archbishop on the 18th October 1950, becoming Archbishop Makarios III at the age of thirty-seven. The election also gave him the status of Ethnarch, i.e. national leader of the Greek people in Cyprus. Because the Archbishop is elected and not appointed, the people therefore elect both their spiritual *and* their national leader; and he represents them in all respects.

Now in this powerful position his fight for Enosis continued on a larger scale. He founded the Pancyprian Youth Organization (PEON) and organized every kind of mass meeting and rally that was large enough to attract the attention of the outside world. With the same aim in view he made long tours visiting Greece, Syria, Egypt and the U.S.A.

In 1952 Colonel Grivas came from Greece to study the possibility of an armed campaign and of smuggling arms into the island; as the outcome of which a shipload of arms and explosives was landed from a Greek caique in March and another in October 1954. The actual starting date of the revolution was delayed by the capture of the caique *Aghios Georghios* with its cargo of arms off the south coast near Khlorakas. But at dawn on April 1, 1955 the armed struggle by the underground guerrillas began with a series of explosives that wrecked police stations and government offices all over the island. Leaflets signed Dighenis, Cyprus's legendary figure which was the pseudonym used by Colonel Grivas, announced the existence of the EOKA organization.

After three months of bomb outrages Britain held a conference in London with Greek and Turkish representatives in an effort to find a settlement that would suit all sides, but no agreement was reached and it led ultimately to anti-Greek riots in Istanbul and Izmir when millions of pounds' worth of Greek property was destroyed. There were retaliations and the London conference was called off. During this time the situation in Cyprus had deteriorated and Field Marshal Sir John Harding, former chief of the Imperial General Staff was brought in as Governor, and more British troops arrived. A state of emergency was proclaimed which gave the Governor the right to impose the death penalty on those possessing arms or explosives and to retain or deport anyone without trial. Sir John Harding was not only the right soldier for the job but his talks with Archbishop Makarios over a draft statement of policy came nearer to an agreement than any of the previous ones had done. However the Colonial Secretary arrived in

February 1956 to discuss this statement, but subsequently the talks broke down and twelve days later the Archbishop was deported to the Seychelles in the Indian Ocean.

A settlement at this time, no matter how inconclusive, would have given the island some form of self government before the main issue was raised again; and also made the opportunity for the Greek and Turkish Cypriots to regain confidence in each other. But with Makarios gone the terrorist activities reached a new peak and the British stepped up their security measures, recruiting Turkish Cypriots into the police force so that now the Greeks who had previously left the Turks alone, began to fight them. Also, it was during this time and the subsequent talks to find a solution, that partition became a concrete aim in the Turkish Cypriot mind. But most important of all, there was now no Greek Cypriot leader for the British to negotiate with and on 28th March 1957 Makarios was released. He was not allowed to return to Cyprus, and he made Athens his headquarters.

The continuous negotiations dragged on through 1958 to 1959 and it became obvious to all concerned that a settlement of some sort must be arrived at. Early in January 1959 the Prime Ministers of Greece and Turkey met in Zurich determined to draw up an outline of a settlement and this was later taken to London to be discussed with the British Government. Finally the three Prime Ministers, together with Archbishop Makarios and Dr Kuchuk the head of the Turkish Cypriot community, met in London. On 19th February 1959, after queries from Makarios, the London Agreements were signed; of which Churchill said: 'They chose the worst'.

Now, with Cyprus to be declared an independent republic, Makarios returned to the island where, needless to say, his reception was rapturous. His fight was over and to every Greek Cypriot he was a liberator.

During the first years of independence, certain clauses in the constitution were considered unworkable by the Greek Cypriots and in 1963 Archbishop Makarios put thirteen amendments to the Turkish Cypriot leadership. They refused to contemplate any change in the constitution as it was laid down. From this came the present impasse for the whole constitution was shelved, leaving the Turkish Cypriots with no say in the running of the island and the Greeks firmly in control.

Archbishop Makarios came to power on his fight for Enosis and now it is becoming increasingly obvious that to contemplate union with Greece makes a permanent deadlock against any settlement between Greek and Turkish Cypriots. Nothing can be done until Cyprus is freed from the dictates of both Greece and Turkey. His Beautitude must surely realize this and want his island to stand on its own feet, enjoy the prosperity that can come its way; and clear up the Turkish Cypriot question which is on the conscience of every fair-minded Greek Cypriot. In the meantime, is it any wonder, in this state of flux, that the Turkish Cypriots stand firm for their demand for partition?

Archbishop Makarios has often been criticized for changing horses in mid-stream, but perhaps it is just common sense when it is not possible to reach the other bank. Whatever may be said – and many vitriolic things are thrown at him – his ability in dealing with his countrymen, the constitution and the interference of the outside world, is immense. Many people's distrust of the Archbishop doesn't go further than their disbelief in the merging of church and politics, but it is inherent in their culture for the church and the secular to be one.

He is, however, a paradox and one is continually being jolted by his impetuous remarks and announcements against the Turks. How can he hope to succeed in joining the two communities after such statements, even if they are under extreme duress?

The American Ambassador's limousine was just driving away from the door. Another equally impressive one was pulling up in front of the large porch. It is certainly a far cry from that small village in the Paphos Hills which lies in the heart of the pagan world of Aphrodite and the churches riddled with tales of miracles. . . .

A young man came towards me, 'Come, Miss Toy,' he said 'His Beautitude will see you now.'

He opened the large doors and stood back. As I passed through, the only occupant in the room rose from behind a large desk and came towards me smiling and holding out both hands. . . .

I had been warned that President Makarios would impress me, that he could 'charm the birds off the trees' and that under the benign manner there was this and that. . . . Everyone had been eager to prepare me – as well they might! It is the magnetism one supposes that has baffled and bluffed even the toughest journalist and politician, despite what they have heard previously. But what is unexpected – and his greatest asset – is the sense of humanity and good-tempered pleasantness, a willingness to be friends.

We sat one on each side of the wide empty desk and I have seldom felt so at ease. What a superb diplomat, for of course he had done his homework and knew all about me. Makarios is good-looking with a fine silky beard, rather fair and with heavily lidded eyes. His voice is beautiful and he speaks soft excellent English. Now I understood the look of frustration on all their faces when they tried to warn me about his charm!

There was a sense of underlying exuberance, almost suppressed excitement which I found difficult to place as he recorded, in fine sequence, his life's story which I in my turn knew. It was only when he came to the part where he had been approached more than once to return to Cyprus that the sequence faltered. Had he ever really contemplated turning his back on this new active life? Perhaps he had, for as he continued, none of the spectacular things, the acclaim, the rise to dizzy heights came into the narrative; or was it that by now he is so immersed that there can be no comment – no escape? Whatever the cause, the excitement had gone out of the voice as though the exuberance of the early struggles is already forgotten. He tackled any near-the-bone question adroitly and with such absence of displeasure that the question unanswered was barely noticed. This experienced, much-travelled man had kept his veneer of simplicity, which is no doubt fortified by his religious discipline. When finally I rose to go he came from behind the desk to wish me a safe journey and to chat a moment longer at the door as though there was little else to do. But outside the waiting-room was full of people – the President's busy morning was taking its course. . . .

18

Departure

'Destroy your house, and with the treasure
hidden in it
You will be able to build a thousand houses.
The treasure lies under it, there is no help
for it;
Hesitate not to pull it down, do not tarry!'
RUMI

I drove across the Mesaoria Plain which was burnt brown now by the summer sun; and when Famagusta came in sight it was glowing like a fire ball. Famagusta – 'Hidden in the Sand'. Belkiss had not been able to come after all; a small son's fever had naturally taken precedence over a jaunt to a friend. The road shimmered in the extreme heat. It was all familiar now and I scarcely noticed the U.N. observation posts and was adept at dodging the more erratic drivers.

I was leaving the next day by ship, the way I had come and over the intervening eight months there had been a gradual easing of tension, a relaxing of restrictions and a seeming return to normal. Now the Turkish Cypriots were free to move in and out of their enclaves, having more vehicles and some trade. Kemel Rustem had even opened a new bookshop over the border into the Greek side in Nicosia and the island was flooded again with tourists who talked with delight of the sunny carefree island – and seldom met a Turk. More and more British arrived to buy up houses and retire in the sun, and any sense of unease was greeted with amazed wonder. True, the Turks still refused to allow the Greeks into their enclaves and insisted on the convoys through their sector. Tiresome as this appears to be, they are not only the minority population but have been systematically weakened as well. Above all, four long years of confinement and deprivation have engendered a 'siege mentality' that will take gentler handling than board-room blustering and growls of impatience, to overcome.

Now there are other rumblings and President Makarios faces

another problem that could turn the Greek–Turkish situation into a vicious circle. True, he seeks a solution with the Turks; for the island has evolved and wants to take its proper place in the world, but he knows no such solution is possible with them until the cry of Enosis is stilled. However it was on this cry that he came to power and there are those who are not going to let him forget it, practical as it may be. So there are all the implications of its becoming a three-sided fight, with the Turks veering more and more for partition against the sparring brothers. Wasn't this, after all, where I came in. . . . ?

Index

Index

Index